*This book is dedicated to
our unique community and its heritage
by the following sponsors:*

AGENCY SERVICES, INC.

Henry and Judy Stansbury

THE ISPA COMPANY

Ron and Anne Kaufman

LOYOLA FEDERAL SAVINGS BANK

Joseph Mosmiller, Chairman

*It has been made available
through the auspices of*

THE CATONSVILLE HISTORICAL SOCIETY

Catonsville
1880 to 1940
From Village To Suburb

by Edward Orser
and Joseph Arnold

University of Maryland
Baltimore County

THE
DONNING COMPANY
PUBLISHERS
NORFOLK/VIRGINIA BEACH

Copyright © 1989 by Edward Orser and Joseph Arnold
Second printing 1995
All rights reserved, including the right to reproduce this work in any form whatsoever without permission in writing from the publisher, except for brief passages in connection with a review. For information, write:

The Donning Company/Publishers,
184 Business Park Drive, Suite 106
Virginia Beach, Virginia   23462

B. L. Walton, Jr., Project Director
Laura Hill, Reprint Research Coordinator
Edited by
Elizabeth B. Bobbitt, Associate Editor
Richard A. Horwege, Senior Editor
Designed by Joan Croyder

Library of Congress Cataloging in Publication Data:

Orser, W. Edward.
    Catonsville, 1880 to 1940: from village to suburb/by Edward
  Orser and Joseph Arnold.
       p.   cm.
       Includes bibliographical references.
       ISBN 0-89865-793-8 (limited ed.)
       1. Catonsville (Md.)—History—Pictorial works. 2. Catonsville
(Md.)—Description—Views. 3. Catonsville (Md.)—History.
I. Arnold, Joseph L. II. Title.
F189.C35O77   1989
975.2'71-dc20   89-23695
                                          CIP

Printed in the United States of America

Contents

Foreword By Jean Walsh 6

Acknowledgments 8

   Chapter I   Catonsville: Created by Many Generations 11

   Chapter II   The Early Village, 1810 to 1880 15
      "A Delightful Summer Retreat" 17

   Chapter III   The Summer Home Era, 1880 to 1900 21
      Catonsville in the 1880 Manuscript Census 25
      Estates and Summer Homes 27
      The Village Center Takes Shape 30
      Frederick Road: Catonsville's "Main Street" 32
      Victorian Elegance: The Eden Terrace Subdivision 38
      Social Life in the 1880s and 1890s 46
      An Estate Family: The Lurmans 52

   Chapter IV   Streetcar Suburb, 1900 to 1920 61
      A Page From the 1910 Manuscript Census 63
      Sanborn Fire Insurance Atlas of Catonsville, 1910 65
      Mapping the 1910 Population 71
      The 1910 Census: Work 81
      The 1910 Census: Place of Origin 86
      The 1910 Census: Race, School, and Homeownership 90
      The Frederick Road Commercial Center, 1910 to 1916 94
      Business Life on Frederick Road 98
      Streetcar Housing Developments, 1900 to 1918 104
      Schooling in the New Century 107
      Social Life in the 1900s and 1910s 112
      A Winters Lane Family: The Coes 117

   Chapter V   The Auto Era, 1920 to 1940 123
      Catonsville Fire Insurance Maps, July 1925 125
      Catonsville Fire Insurance Maps, March 1930 127
      The Village Center, 1920 to 1940 130
      Business Life in the 1920s and 1930s 135
      Building Homes in Catonsville: The Mohler Brothers 138
      Summit Park 140
      Holmehurst 144
      Somerset Group Homes 146
      Catonsville's Churches 147
      High School Life 150
      Life in Boom Times and Hard Times 154
      A Frederick Road Family: The Harmons 160

   Chapter VI   Beyond 1940 167

Bibliography 171

Index 173

About the Authors 176

Foreword

Before descriptive words were printed, read, and retained about Catonsville in its own local newspaper, and before families obtained photographic equipment or professional photographs, little record of our area's history was preserved, except through such traditional sources as letters, church reports, art, legal documents, government records (like the federal census), and physical structures. However, with the introduction of cameras in the latter years of the nineteenth century, and the advent of the Catonsville weekly newspaper in 1881, visual images and printed records of noteworthy actions, opinions, and experiences of Catonsvillians became a tangible reality, helping us in the present day to reconstruct those early times. Thus, the period from the 1880s onward is a rich one for the documentary history of a community like Catonsville, and it is this period that the present volume illustrates so well.

Catonsville's progress into new avenues of improvement started in the 1880s, a period which was notable for its inventions and its scientific and engineering discoveries. Electricity became a major power source; communication and transportation took forward leaps. Individuals witnessed more advances in the next sixty years than in any previous or subsequent period. This pictorial history provides a vivid chronicle of the significant era in Catonsville's transition from rural village to metropolitan suburb.

Under the able direction of Dr. Edward Orser

and Dr. Joseph Arnold, the students at the University of Maryland Baltimore County who participated in the Catonsville History Project, ferreted out the significant data from a variety of documentary sources to reconstruct the social history of the community, deducing trends of development and change. This scholarly work culminated in UMBC's popular 1988 exhibit, a valuable contribution to the community and the basis for this book. For those of us who have long been interested and involved in learning and disseminating local history, the project was the impetus for us to participate in the preparation of this chronicle.

This book, we believe, will be attractive and interesting, not only to the persons who have known and enjoyed Catonsville for many years, but also to newcomers who will establish roots here.

The Catonsville Historical Society is delighted to have sponsored this publication. Membership in the society and in the Friends of the Catonsville Library would be a fulfilling adjunct to the reader's enthusiasm for Catonsville history which, we anticipate, will be aroused by this book. Let us enjoy and preserve Catonsville's heritage, while continuing to make advances for the betterment of "our village" and surrounding suburban communities.

Jean S. Walsh

Acknowledgments

The effort that has culminated in this book has been a collaborative one between the Catonsville community and the University of Maryland Baltimore County (UMBC). The rich reservoir of documents and photographs on Catonsville's history has been preserved and made available primarily by the Friends of the Catonsville Library and also by the Catonsville Historical Society, as well as by many private family collections. The university, through the Catonsville History Project which we have had the pleasure of directing, lent the expertise of its faculty, staff, and students to produce a major exhibit on the community in the fall of 1988. That exhibition has been revised to form the basis of this book.

A third important factor in this enterprise has been the support of the local businesses which have provided the financial sponsorship for this book. We deeply appreciate their faith in the project and recognize them here: Agency Services, Inc. (Henry H. Stansbury, President); Catonsville Plumbing and Heating Co., Inc. (Timothy C. Kraus, President); Consolidated Insurance Center, Inc. (John F. Doetzer, President, and Thomas F. Campion, Executive Vice President); ISPA Company (Ronald Kaufman, President); Loyola Federal Savings and Loan Association (Joseph W. Mosmiller, Chairman); Whalen Properties (Stephen W. Whalen, Jr., President).

This volume represents a legacy to be shared by interested readers today, and we hope that it will serve future generations as a pictorial record of an important era in the transition of Catonsville from a rural village to a modern suburb.

The project originally began in a UMBC classroom in the belief that our students might develop their research skills as they assisted us in examining and interpreting the history of Baltimore area communities. For the project on the history of Catonsville we worked together as a team, poring over the federal manuscript censuses, combing the newspaper on microfilm, searching photographic collections, and asking many questions of current Catonsville residents. For their efforts much credit is due to the student participants: Ken Arrington, Marc Berman, Suzanne Gasser, Mary Gerstenberger, Kelly Grace Gilberto, Gerry Hughes, Elizabeth Lacy, Patrick McGregor, Linda Rayman, and Paula Romey.

The major repository for the history of the community is the Catonsville Room, at the Catonsville Area Branch of the Baltimore County Public Library, maintained by the Friends of the Catonsville Library. Many photographs and other documents in the book are from its excellent collection. In addition to Francis E. Old, manager of the Catonsville Branch, and William Keegan, past president of the Friends, we would like to express our appreciation to the volunteers of the Catonsville Room who have worked diligently to develop the collection and whose efforts greatly aid all who are interested in the community's past. Especially, we would like to single out the following who have been generous in sharing their knowledge and offering their assistance throughout the project: Elizabeth Grim, Ralph Heidelbach, Laura Kapraun, Elizabeth Peddicord, Pamela Seng, and Lisa Vicari.

Equally supportive of the project has been the Catonsville Historical Society and its president Eugene Adams. The society's willingness to endorse the book project was essential in making its publication possible. The society was organized in 1973 after the Townsend property at 1824 Frederick Road was bequeathed in trust for a historical society. Its publications committee has assisted greatly in helping to edit the manuscript and checking for historical accuracy. For their tireless efforts in this regard, sincere thanks are due to Elizabeth Grim, Ralph Heidelbach, Elizabeth Peddicord, and Jean Walsh. Committee members Henry Stansbury and Jean Walsh played a key role in convincing the book's financial sponsors to support the project, and Mark Silvestri, Bea McComas, and Henry Stansbury accepted responsibility for promotion and distribution.

Jean Walsh, author of the foreword to this volume, has made a significant contribution to the efforts of both organizations over the years, diligently seeking out records of the community's past, and writing her weekly newspaper columns on historical events. We all owe her a debt of gratitude for her dedication and energy in preserving Catonsville history.

Special thanks are also due to Catonsville residents who contributed photographs and other documents from their family collections and permitted their inclusion in this book: Mae Esther Coe, Earl Dew, Burch Harmon, Antoinette Lawrence Hughes, James Mohler, Elizabeth Peddicord, Dorothy Maisel Reis, John Schatz, Ann Steffens, and Jean Walsh.

The project also owes a great debt of gratitude

to the University of Maryland Baltimore County for the support afforded the project, including the funding for the exhibit which preceded this book publication. President Michael Hooker, Provost Adam Yarmolinsky, and Associate Vice-President John Starr all recognized the value of such campus-community cooperation and have been warm and generous advocates.

For outstanding technical assistance in the preparation of this volume, Alan Scherr, who made the photographic copy prints, and Carolyn Ferrigno, typist and editor for the manuscript, have made invaluable contributions. Joe School of UMBC Cartographic Services designed the very fine census distribution maps.

Since the book grows out of the exhibit which appeared at the UMBC Library in 1988, it is appropriate to single out a number of individuals who contributed to the exhibit production and presentation: Patti Pace, coordinator, and Paula Sloane and Whitney Sherman, designers; Billy Wilkinson, director of the Albin O. Kuhn Library and Gallery at UMBC; and William Dunlop, coordinator of the gallery.

Finally, we appreciate the courtesy extended by the following institutions and individuals for permission to use illustrations and documents from their collections: Bafford Photographic Collection, Albin O. Kuhn Library, UMBC; Baltimore Streetcar Museum Collection; McKeldin Library, University of Maryland College Park; Boston Museum of Fine Arts; Library of Congress; National Archives (special thanks to Angie Spicer); and Jacques Kelly.

All photo and document credits are noted in the captions.

Castle Thunder was the home of Richard Caton, for whom Catonsville was named. The house stood on the site of the present Catonsville Area Branch of the Baltimore County Public Library, Frederick Road and Beaumont Avenue. Catonsville Room

CHAPTER 1

Catonsville: Created by Many Generations

Catonsville is the creation of thousands of different people through many decades and generations. Their marks on the local landscape can still be seen in large patterns and small remnants.

Many of these reminders pre-date the important decades of change which began in the 1880s. Frederick Road still serves as the community's main thoroughfare. Long the route of the westward road, in 1805 the state legislature designated it as the Frederick Turnpike (superseding the earlier county-owned turnpike), a privately controlled franchise until its sale to the state in 1910. The horsecar tracks laid on its roadbed in 1862 were replaced by trolley tracks in 1895, and these too have disappeared, but the residential and commercial developments they spawned remain very much in evidence. Even though Richard Caton's Castle Thunder was torn down in 1906, its property lines, surveyed in 1810, are still reflected in the unusual angle of all the present streets on the north side of Frederick Road from Winters Lane to Wyndcrest Avenue; these lines in turn had been derived from colonial land grants. The name of Fusting Avenue is a reminder of Joseph P. Fusting, credited as the founder of Catonsville in 1829, one of the town's major nineteenth-century businessmen and the local agent of the horsecar line.

The churches also recall some of this early his-

Catonsville: Created by Many Generations

tory. St. Timothy's, founded in 1844, served many of the elite summer residents as well as local members. German Protestants built the rustic chapel for the Salem Lutheran Church in 1849, the structure now referred to as Historic Old Salem. Roman Catholics of German and Irish background worshiped first at St. Agnes, beginning in 1852, then established a second parish, called St. Mark, in 1888. Their stone church (now the chapel) was placed near the heart of Catonsville. The present sanctuary for Grace African Methodist Episcopal Church was not built until 1912, but its congregation traces its roots to 1869 and it stands on the site of two earlier wooden edifices, a reminder of the long history of Catonsville's black community. Catonsville Methodists erected the first of two structures pre-dating the present facility in 1857, and Catonsville Presbyterians (their early sanctuary now accommodating the Christadelphian Church) formed a congregation in 1881. While hardly a complete list of Catonsville's churches, these early institutions and structures not only evoke the village's religious history, but provide clues to its formative settlement patterns.

By mid-century the village and its surrounding countryside along the historic heights once known generally as the Hunting Ridge had also attracted a wealthy elite, who built permanent mansions and extravagant summer houses, where they might escape the heat and the increasingly dense population of nearby Baltimore City. The Summit Apartment House and the Catonsville Community College Administration Building, formerly Hilton, still serve as impressive reminders that they were once the large nineteenth-century estates of the Gary and Glenn families, while nearby Catonsville High School occupies the site of the Lurmans' Farmlands, its carefully planted woods and grounds reminders of the era of the estates.

Important as Catonsville's early years may have been in shaping its future, it was during the period from 1880 to 1940 that Catonsville made the dramatic and significant transition from rural village to modern suburb. In 1880 Catonsville consisted of a small crossroads community serving the needs of travelers along the Frederick Turnpike, the shops and residences of a growing number of merchants and artisans, and the surrounding countryside shared by working farms and scattered spacious estates. By 1940 Catonsville had become a sector of the Baltimore metropolitan area, many of its residents now commuters linked by streetcar and auto to employment and shopping throughout the city, its business district serving a large region of Baltimore County (though about to be eclipsed by post-World War II shopping center competition), and its upland spaces the site of a variety of residential developments. Catonsville residents of 1940 still envisioned their community as a town, still enjoyed its remaining open spaces, and still thought of Catonsville as distinct from the City; nevertheless, the foundation for its contemporary metropolitan suburban character had been set by the time of World War II.

The story of Catonsville between 1880 and 1940 is not so much a history of estates and first families as it is one of business development, residential expansion, and the lives of countless ordinary citizens who created the social character of the new Catonsville and established a pattern of living in a thriving and changing community. Reminders of this part of Catonsville's story are still quite evident in the commercial center along Frederick Road, in spite of the many changes the years have wrought. Wilson and Poehlman, the lumber and coal business of the late nineteenth century, became John S. Wilson Company, though the Wilsons are no longer connected with the firm. Whitney's Meat Market and Grim's Bakery were typical of the businesses which purveyed their products for over half a century, though they are now remembered by fewer and fewer present-day residents. The splendid facade of Heidelbach's Grocery is still discernible above the sign for the building's current tenant, the Plymouth Wallpaper Company. Other important remnants have all but disappeared. Catonsville's firehouse, at Frederick Road and Egges Lane, stands where once the patrons of the Railroad Hotel sipped Eigenbrot's lager beer. Across the street was the depot of the Catonsville Short-Line Passenger Railroad, whose steam trains to Baltimore in 1884 ushered in the era of power-driven commuter travel that unalterably changed the future of the village, though even more dramatic was the subsequent impact of

Catonsville: Created by Many Generations

electrified trolleys in the 1890s and the advent of the gasoline auto in the twentieth century. Now the depot, the Railroad Hotel, and Eigenbrot's beer are all gone. Today, the Short Line Railroad has vanished, its only trace visible where its former roadbed crosses busy commuter streets. Nevertheless, the railroad, the streetcars, and the old hotels and shops of the late nineteenth and early twentieth centuries played important roles in creating the modern suburb of Catonsville by turning a semi-rural crossroads into a thriving village.

Catonsville's story of change is equally evident in its residential development. Beginning in the 1880s on a substantial scale, and continuing through the period in eras of boom and bust, Catonsville's middle-income builders subdivided the old estates, farmlands, woods, and open spaces, creating the housing variety that has left its physical stamp indelibly on the residential character of the community. As developers sought both to create a market and to respond to it, each project became a business calculation with tremendous import in terms of the type of resident who would be attracted. Their dreams and estimates helped shape the kind of community Catonsville would become. From the elite developments of Oak Forest Park or Eden Terrace to the many more modest sections of cottages, bungalows and rowhouses, developers and builders like Cone, Gerwig, Hubner, Maisel, the Mohler brothers, and the Schatz brothers (to mention only a few representative names) were essential to the establishment of Catonsville as a modern suburb.

At the center of all these changes, of course, are the people of the town. Generation after generation not only played a role in the physical development of the community, but fashioned its social institutions, creating new social networks and habits. No fact about the period from 1880 to 1940 is more significant than the area's dramatic population growth. In 1880 Catonsville numbered approximately 309 households (registered in the federal manuscript census of that year); by 1940 population in Baltimore County's first district (of which Catonsville occupied a major portion) stood at 21,221, approximately 5,000 households, an index of exponential growth. Change of such magnitude required countless adjustments, resilience, and adaptability. As they refashioned old institutions and created new ones—churches, clubs, social organizations, community events—Catonsville's residents created a pattern of life for themselves more suburban than village-like. Change was not without challenge and problems; nor was it always accepted. For example, the racial division of the community was as evident in 1940 as it had been in 1880. Continuity and change thus are equally important themes in the social history of this important period of Catonsville's development.

It is easier to depict the history of first families and major entrepreneurs, more difficult to do justice to the full story of an entire community. Yet, no picture of Catonsville's evolution from village to suburb is complete without a comprehensive view of all its people: rich and poor, native and foreign-born, black and white, male and female. While the story which follows tries to be as inclusive as the documents permit, it must inevitably be selective and less than thorough. Therefore, highlights on the experience of four representative families—the Lurmans, Coes, Mohlers, and Harmons—are included to illustrate the diversity, resilience, and integrity of individual lives in the community during this era of stability and change. Neither more nor less important than other families of the epoch, these four provide a visual legacy that personalizes the meaning of life in the Catonsville of 1880 to 1940.

The brief glimpse of Catonsville offered in these pages attempts to give attention both to the material and human sides of the town, illustrating the previous physical landscapes and social worlds of Catonsville and the lives of the people who helped to create them. The major focus is upon the 1880 to 1940 period when Catonsville changed from a rural village into one of Baltimore County's largest suburbs. Hopefully these old maps, photos, census materials, advertisements, and newspaper articles will provide a deeper appreciation of the long, complex process of metropolitan growth and community change so well illustrated by the history of Catonsville.

"Election Scene at Catonsville" (Maryland), 1845, by Alfred Jacob Miller (1810-1874) was drawn with pencil and wash and heightened with white on brown paper.
M. and M. Karolik Collection; courtesy, Museum of Fine Arts, Boston

CHAPTER II

The Early Village, 1810 to 1880

The early name "Catonville" derives from Richard Caton, who in 1810 was commissioned by his father-in-law, Charles Carroll of Carrollton, to develop a large plot of land on the north and south sides of the recently rechartered Frederick Turnpike somewhat to the east of the colonial-era Rolling Road. Situated seven miles west of Baltimore on the crest of a broad ridge, this was a natural location for the establishment of a village.

During the nineteenth century, turnpike travelers moving west out of Baltimore climbed slowly to an altitude of over five hundred feet above the city before reaching the village, called Catonsville after the "s" was added sometime around 1830. Just beyond the settlement they faced a sharp descent into the Patapsco River Valley at Ellicott's Mills. Thus by the 1830s and 1840s, Catonsville had become a popular stopping place for wagons and stagecoaches.

By the Civil War era the village's airy location had begun to attract two types of people who formed the community. One group was composed of businessmen and artisans who developed a small commercial strip along the Frederick Turnpike. They provided teamsters and stagecoach passengers with taverns, blacksmiths, and wagon repair shops. Their stores served these travelers as well as the local residents and farmers in the surrounding countryside. The other group attracted to the area consisted of wealthy Baltimoreans who, from the 1850s onwards, surrounded the village with country estates. Most of these mansions were occupied only in the summer when the heat of the city drove its elite families out to a more salubrious atmosphere; but some families began to

The Early Village 1810 to 1880

stay all year—traveling into the city by private carriage or, after 1862, by the Frederick Road horsecar line.

Very gradually, from the 1880s onwards, these two strikingly different communities merged into the modern suburb of Catonsville.

In the Baltimore Sun, *November 27, 1862, the horsecar line out to Catonsville was called a "railroad" because its incorporators hoped to use steam engines, but the owners of the Frederick Turnpike refused. The line ended at the Terminal Hotel, located on Frederick Road just beyond South Rolling Road.*

A horsecar headed in the direction of Catonsville along Frederick Road passes the old entrance to the Loudon Park Cemetery in Irvington in the late nineteenth century. The car bears the names of intermediate stops at Carrollton, Irvington, and Paradise, as well as the car's downtown route along Pratt, Lombard, and Liberty streets to Baltimore Street. This cemetery gateway was built in the 1850s, but eventually demolished for the present structures.
Catonsville Room

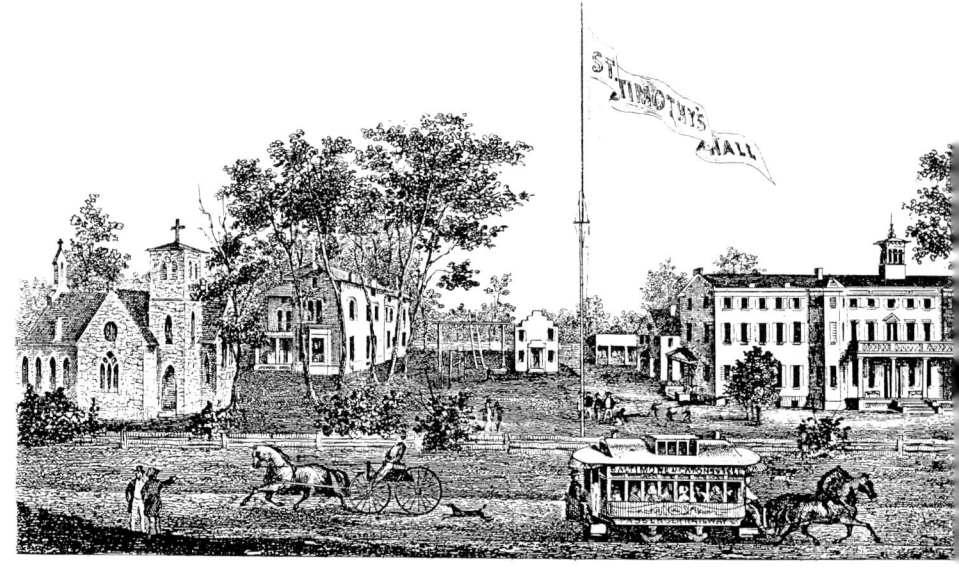

A Catonsville to Baltimore horsecar shortly after the completion of the line in 1862; electric trolleys replaced the horsecars in 1890s. This engraving shows St. Timothy's Hall, which burned in 1872, on the right, and St. Timothy's Episcopal Church, which dates from 1844, on the left. The rectory, erected in 1861, is located between the church and the small structure which is still in use in 1989 with a different roof line. The artistic license of the engraver is evident in the foreshortened area between the buildings and the horsecar on Frederick Road.
Catonsville Room

From an article in the Baltimore *Sun*, July 2, 1881:

Catonsville in Summer

Delightful Suburban Retreat— The Buckboards Are Out

As soon as the girls make their appearance on the roads in those pretty single and double light wood buck-boards that give such pleasant travel in the country, Catonsville feels that the signal has been given to awaken for the summer, and accordingly bestirs herself in the way of festivities befitting the event. Every afternoon nowadays the roads of the village and vicinity are alive with pretty traps and carts bearing prettier girls in prettiest gowns.... The afternoon and evening driving is one of the characteristic customs of the delightful retreat for fashionable Baltimoreans and the young people, many of whom have come to be skillful drivers, have explored all kinds of out-of-the-way, but romantic spots by the help of their easy-going buck-boards and gentle steed, while variety in Catonsville scenery is often found in long drives over beautiful roads as far as Franklintown and Elk Ridge. In the early evening the young wives and daughters often drive down to the depot to meet the 4:56, or "husbands' train," which brings the men of business back to their country homes, whose charms never seem greater than after the heat and dust of the city....

Indeed, life in general at Catonsville is not unlike the ideal English country life ... While there are always many new visitors every summer, and more this season than ever before, it is said, the majority of Catonsvillians, properly speaking, are old residents who have beautiful country seats that have become identified with the place and with the families living in them in some cases for several generations. And then, too, the summer or transient visitor who comes once to the place usually comes again and yet again with the result that every one knows every one else, and Catonsville social life is like a little bit, but a very choice bit, of city social life transplanted, root and branch, to more congenial soil for the summer growth. Hospitable people are the Catonsvillians, and the entertaining, though informal, is only more delightful on that account....

Nearly all of the summer residents are occupied now, and the unoccupied ones will be filled in a few weeks. Among some of the well-known Baltimoreans who are enjoying Catonsville life this summer are Dr. and Mrs. Macgill, Dr. Charles Macgill and the Misses Loulie and Margie Macgill, who live at the beautiful old country place "Eureka," Mr. and Mrs. Henry James, Misses Amy and Emma James, Mr. and Mrs. N. W. James of "Sunnyholme;" Mr. and Mrs. Allan McLane, Jr., Mr. and Mrs. Wm. B. Wilson, of "Glen Alpine;" Mr. and Mrs. James A. Gary and the Misses Gary, of "Maple Lawn;" Mr. and Mrs. Charles Goldsborough, Misses Mary and Ella Goldsborough, of "Bellevue;" Mr. and Mrs. Theodore Lurman, of "Farmlands;" Dr. and Mrs. Samuel Theobald, the Missees Theobald and Mr. Samuel Theobald, Jr., Mr. and Mrs. James Winchester, Mr. and Mrs. John C. George, Miss Etta George, Rev. Thomas Punnett, rector of St. Timothy's; the Misses Punnett, Mr. and Mrs. Graham Bowdoin, Mr. and Mrs. Harry White, of "The Lodge;" Mr. and Mrs. John Gill, Miss Olivia Gill of "Kenwood;" Mr. and Mrs. Gustav Lurman, Misses Lizzie and Fannie Lurman, Miss Mollie Cromwell, Messers. Kennedy, Hamond and John Cromwell, William Taylor, Isaac McKim and John Glenn, Mr. and Mrs. William Deford, Mr. F. M. Colston, Mr. and Mrs. Geo. Gaither, Mr. and Mrs. Robert Garrett, of "Uplands;" Mr. Hollins McKim, Miss Margaret McKim, Mr. John Hubner, Mr. and Mrs. B. N. Baker, Mr. and Mrs. Samuel B. Hough, the Misses Carter, Mr. and Mrs. Frank Albert, Mr. and Mrs. J. T. Albert, Mr. and Mrs. S. S. Lee, General and Mrs. Clinton P. Paine, Colonel and Mrs. Thomas Symington, Mr. and Mrs. Blanchard Randall, Mr. and Mrs. Harry Ranson, and Messrs. Henry and Louis Keidel.

"A Delightful Suburban Retreat"

Homewood, depicted here in 1900 when it was the residence of Henry Keidel, was built for Joseph P. Fusting, one of the chief founders of Catonsville in the antebellum period. He resided there until 1864. The house still stands at 717 Edmondson Avenue.
Jean Walsh

Newburg Hall was an early center of Catonsville social and political life and continued in use until it was razed in 1903 for the construction of Salem Lutheran Church. A restaurant and saloon occupied the first floor, with public halls and meeting rooms on the two upper floors. In the late 1880s the saloon was supplanted by the Women's Christian Temperance Union reading room, where non-alcoholic beverages were served.
Jean Walsh

"A Delightful Suburban Retreat"

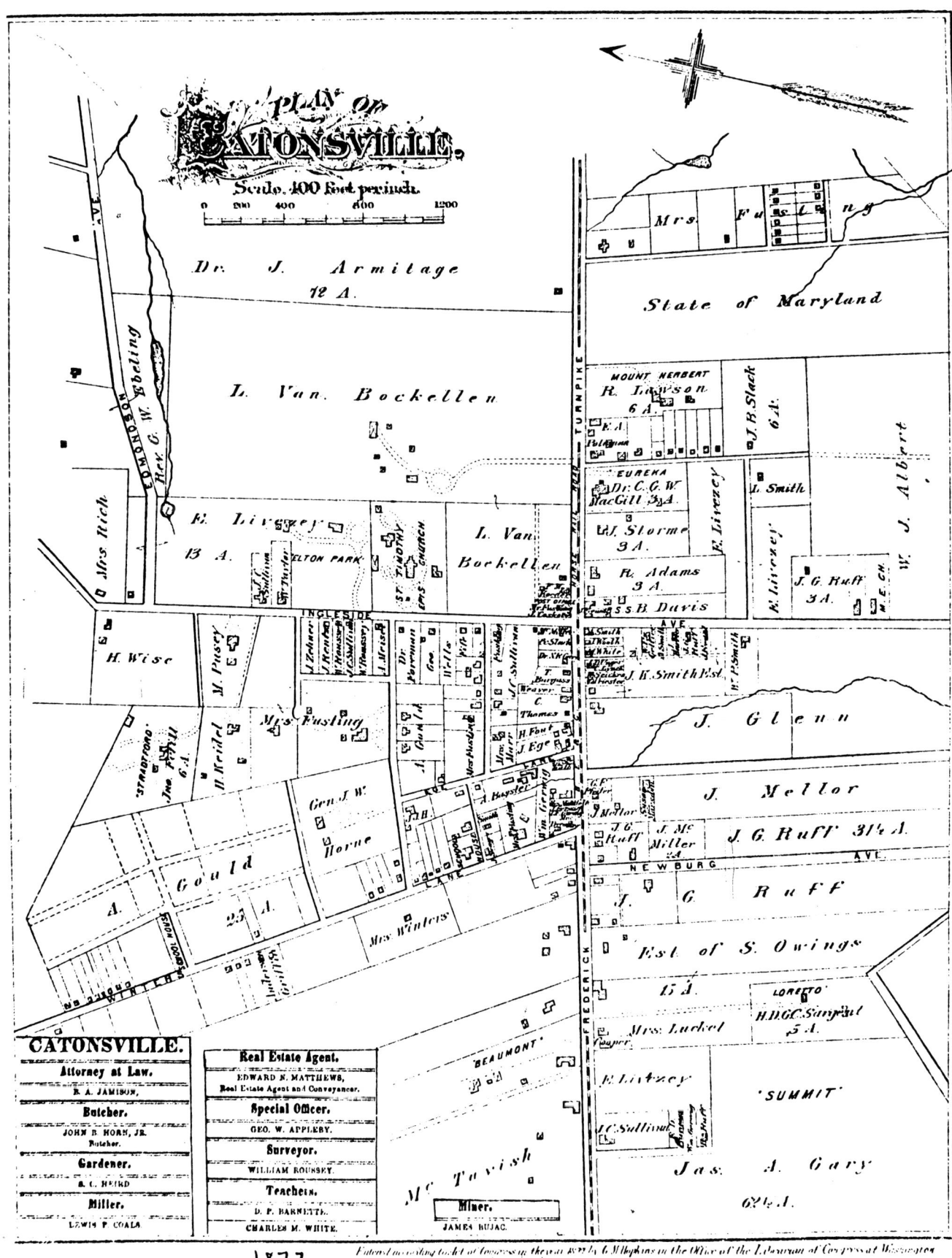

G. M. Hopkins, "Plan of Catonsville," 1877.

The Argus, *April 26, 1890, listed seven daily passenger departures on the Short Line Railroad from its Catonsville depot to Baltimore's Calvert Station.*

THE ARGUS.

PUBLISHED EVERY SATURDAY.

Time Table of the Catonsville Short-Line Railroad.

Leave Catonsville, (Weekdays)
At 6.30, 8.23 and 10.35 a. m., 3.49, 5.38, 7.12 and 10.10 p. m.

On Sunday 9.05, a. m., 1.30, 4.37 and 6.40 p. m.

Leave Calvert Station. Balto., (Weekdays)
At 7.45 and 9.30, a. m., 3.12. 4.35, 6.35, 9.15 and 11.15 p. m.

On Sunday 10.05 a. m., 2.40, 5.35 and 10.05 p. m.

ST. MARK'S NEW CATHOLIC CHURCH

CHAPTER III

The Summer Home Era, 1880 to 1900

Early in the 1880s historian J. Thomas Scharf described Catonsville as an area of "highly cultivated estates," the country residence of "numerous merchants of Baltimore City" and "one of the most beautiful and healthful villages in the State."

In many ways the estates and summer homes set the social tone for the village. Newspaper notices alerted the community to the seasonal openings and closings of summer homes by prominent families whose permanent residences were located in prestigious sections near Baltimore's center. Their presence created employment for artisan and working-class residents, black and white.

Development efforts in the 1880s and 1890s sought to capitalize upon this image as an elite suburb. They ushered in a new period of growth, making these the take-off years for the new Catonsville.

The completion of the Catonsville Short Line Railroad in 1884 and access to electrified streetcar lines on Frederick Road and on Edmondson Avenue by the late 1890s brought Catonsville much more within reach of the growing Baltimore area. Victor Bloede's Eden Terrace development represented a dramatic attempt to attract affluent suburban residents, but equally significant was the erection of more modest cottages by smaller, independent builders who catered to people with average means.

In the same decade that Catonsville was linked by the railroad, it also welcomed its first newspaper, *The Argus* (1881), established by some of the same investors who financed the Short Line

Plan of Catonsville from the Bromley Atlas of 1898

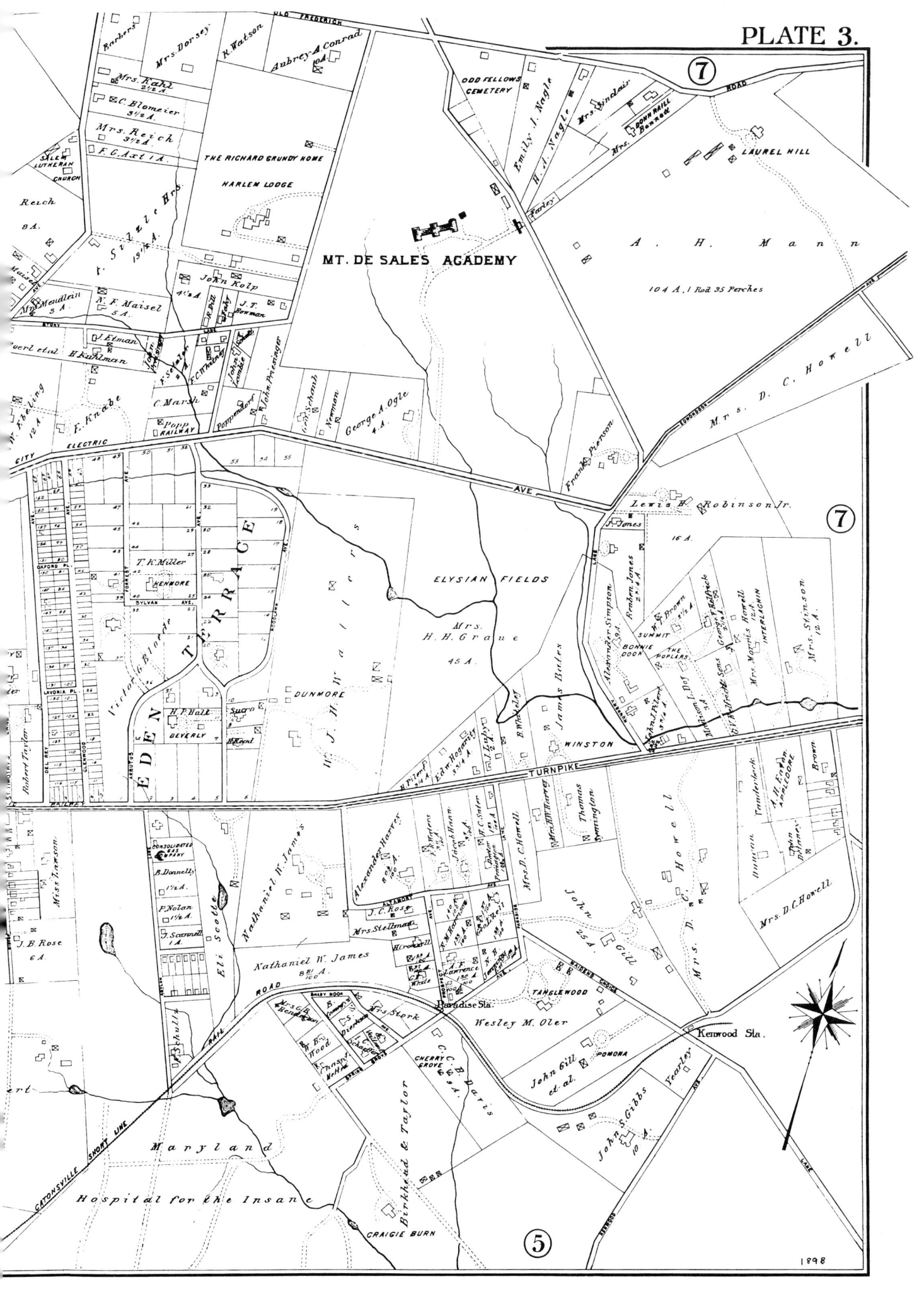

The Summer Home Era, 1880 to 1900

and believed both would spur development. The erection of Library Hall, the formation of local social and political clubs, street expansion—all symbolized the changing era.

German lineage made a distinct imprint upon the Catonsville of this period, evident not only in the Teutonic architectural lines of Library Hall and the office of *The Argus*, but also in the fact that one of every four heads of households was German-born. German ethnicity was a strong component in the establishment of St. Mark Catholic Church and Salem Lutheran Church.

Already the concentration of the community's black population along Winters Lane had been established. Initially attracted to the area to work as cooks, butlers, gardeners, and maids on the large estates, black residents during this period created vital institutions for their community life, such as churches and fraternal organizations.

Electrification of the Frederick Road horsecar line in 1895 (the No. 8), followed shortly in 1899 by completion of electrified service along Edmondson Avenue on the line from Baltimore City to Ellicott City (the No. 14 to Catonsville Junction; the No. 9 all the way to the Patapsco River community), resulted in shorter travel time, reduced fare charges, and more frequent service—one car every twelve minutes during rush hour on the No. 8, for example. These developments brought a swift end to passenger trains on the Short Line Railroad, which, however, continued to haul freight until 1972.

Transportation convenience and economy made Catonsville much more accessible to middle income settlers. By the turn of the century the summer home elite may have set the social standard for Catonsville, but the future lay with the residents of cottages and bungalows. The rural retreat was being rapidly transformed.

Waldeck, built in 1878 at 736 Edmondson Avenue, was formerly the Gustav Gieske home, and is presently the Sterling Ashton Funeral Home.
Catonsville Room

Catonsville in the 1880 Manuscript Census

Michael Raab and his two daughters, Rose and Kate, pause for a photographer in the side yard of their home at 914 Frederick Road, circa 1895.
Catonsville Room

The manuscript census, listing every man, woman, and child, was the basis from which the published census returns were compiled. Illustrated above is the census enumerator's listing of the Thomas H. Boston family in 1880; their descendants still live in the Winters Lane section of Catonsville. The census ledger identified individuals by race and sex: B = black, W = white, M = male, F = female.

25

Catonsville in the 1880 Manuscript Census

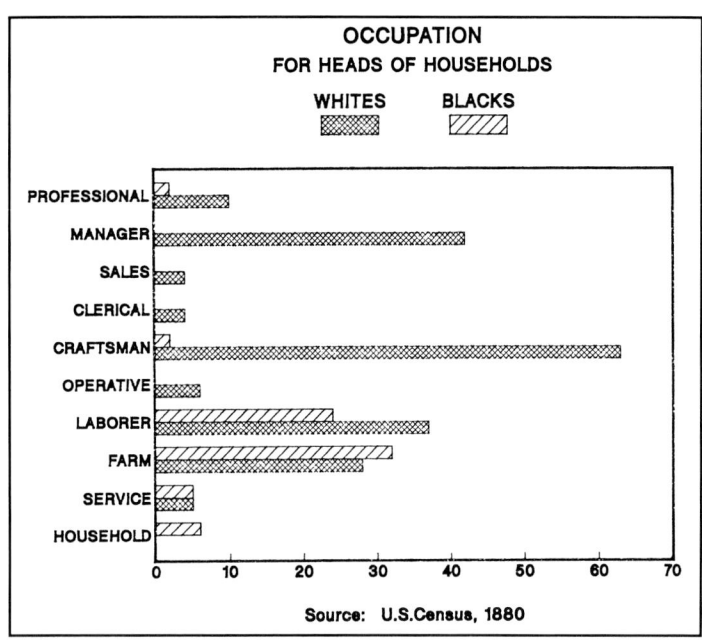

For white household heads, leading occupational categories were: craftsmen (skilled trades), managers (entrepreneurs and business supervisors), and unskilled or common laborers. Farming ranked fourth, but it clearly was declining in importance as a source of employment.

For black household heads, farm labor actually ranked first, with common labor second; both were unskilled job categories, usually among the lower paid.

Most household heads, as listed by the census, were male.
Catonsville History Project, UMBC

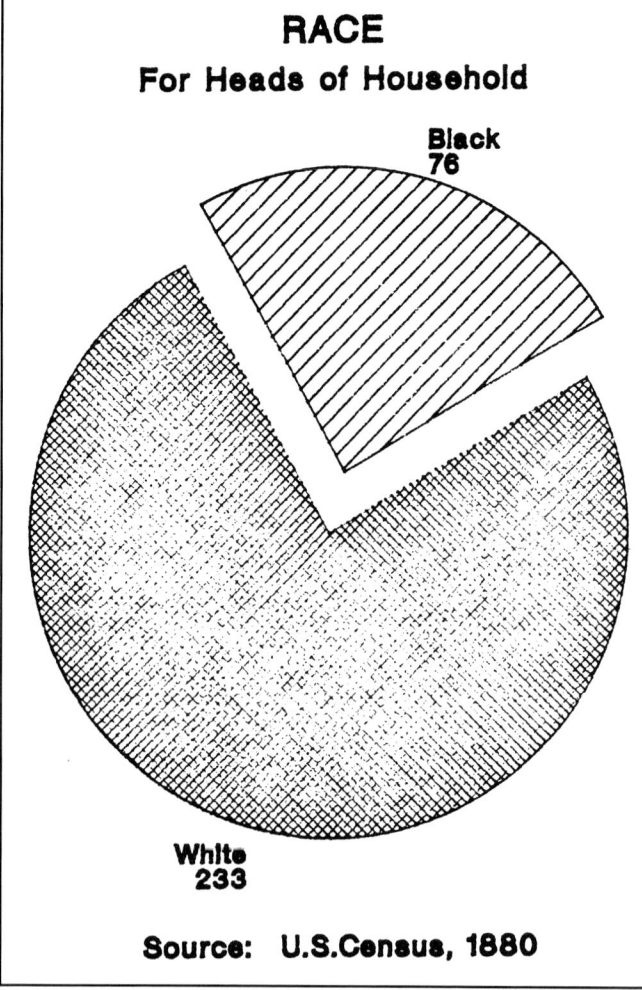

The manuscript census of 1880 listed 25 percent of Catonsville's 309 heads of household as black. These statistics were compiled by Linda Rayman from the U.S. manuscript census for Catonsville.
Catonsville History Project, UMBC

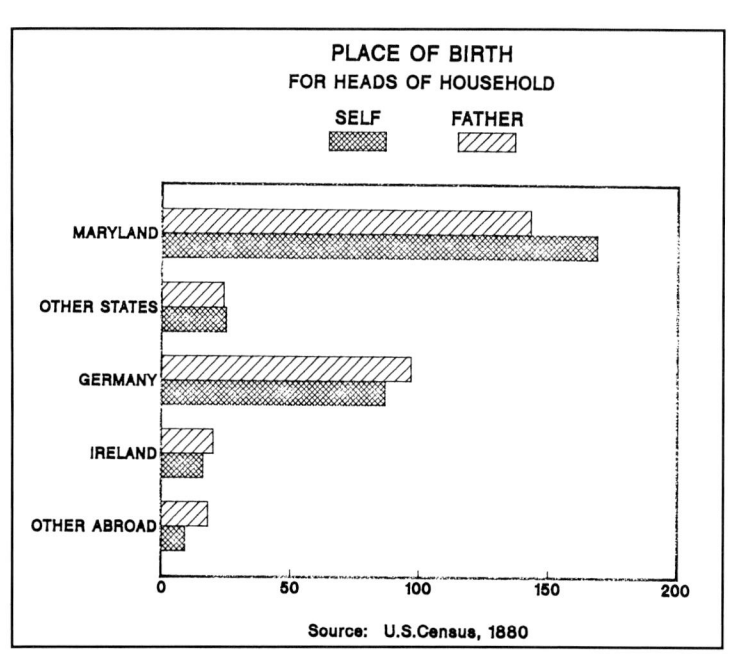

In 1880, 37 percent of all household heads in Catonsville had been born abroad, 25 percent in Germany. Forty-five percent had fathers who had been born outside the United States.
Catonsville History Project, UMBC

Social notices in *The Argus* included the opening of summer homes in Catonsville by families who spent their winters in Baltimore. Such notices appeared until the First World War. The "Personal Mention" column from *The Argus*, April 9, 1910, contained a number of seasonal home openings:

—Mr. and Mrs. Robert T. McDowell have reopened their country home on the Rolling road, after spending the winter months in the city.
—Miss Annie Kennard and her sister, Mrs. Webb, have opened "Kenlouma," their country home on Frederick avenue after spending the winter in Baltimore....
—Mr. and Mrs. William W. Symington entertained a number of friends Saturday evening at the Pot and Kettle Club at dinner. An elaborate menu was served, and about 20 guests were present....
—Major and Mrs. John Sears Gibbs, who have recently returned from the South, have opened, "Searsleigh," their country home at Catonsville, where they will spend the spring and summer....
—Mr. Jerome F. Blome and family opened their country home at Oak Forest Park Thursday.
—Mr. W. H. Surratt of Baltimore has leased the cottage on Beechwood avenue just vacated by Mr. E. H. Donaldson.
—Mr. Leroy Oldham has opened his home on Fusting avenue for the summer after spending the winter in Baltimore.
—Mr. and Mrs. H. B. Davis have opened their country home at Eden Terrace for the summer....

Belle Grove was sketched in 1881 when it was owned by D. C. Howell. It consisted of forty-two acres of land fronting Frederick Road. The mansion today is surrounded by houses built after World War II and sits at the end of a cul-de-sac off Belle Grove Road. This sketch was included in Thomas Scharf's History of Baltimore City and County *(1881).*

Estates and Summer Homes

Summit was the estate of Catonsville's most prominent summer resident, James A. Gary, who served as postmaster general under President William McKinley from 1897 to 1898. The photo appeared in D. B. Perkins, Picturesque Catonsville (1895).
Catonsville Room

Estates and Summer Homes

The Summit mansion sat on a hundred-acre tract on the south side of Frederick Road west of the village center. Since the 1920s it has served as an apartment house.
Catonsville Room

The Village Center Takes Shape

Three structures which symbolized the new vitality of village life in the 1880s stood side by side: Wilson and Poehlman (lumber and coal dealers), Library Hall (which also housed the Catonsville Post Office at this time), and the Catonsville Short Line Railroad depot. The railway line from Baltimore to Catonsville was completed in 1884.
Catonsville Room

The Village Center Takes Shape

Library Hall, built in 1887, was used extensively for public meetings, social events, and theatrical productions. In 1897 the newly organized First National Bank of Catonsville occupied the front area, which formerly had housed the Post Office. The Hall is shown here circa 1900.
Catonsville Room

Wilson and Poehlman, circa, 1885.
Catonsville Room

Frederick Road: Catonsville's "Main Street"

Whitney's Meat Market at 723 Frederick Road was manned by, left to right, Messrs. Whitney, Poehlman, and Gardner, who operated the shop at the turn of the century.
Catonsville Room

Largest, Cleanest, Most Sanitary Meat Market in Catonsville.

When folks comment on the fine firmness and juiciness of our Meats we explain that our cold-storage refrigerators, coupled with our care in buying only the best, have all to do with it.

Our cold-storage plant works night and day for our customers.

Prime meat headquarters.

WHITNEY'S MEAT MARKET
723 FREDERICK AVENUE,

Advertisement in The Argus, June 17, 1899.

Frederick Road: Catonsville's "Main Street"

Hoffman's blacksmith shop at 713 Frederick Road. William S. Hoffman is shown here at his forge in the 1930s. It was a busier place in the 1890s, before the advent of the automobile. On the floor above, Bauman's carriage repair shop could be reached by a ramp at the rear of the building. Shortly after this photo was taken, Mr. Hoffman gave up his business and the building was converted into a beauty parlor on the first floor and offices upstairs.
Catonsville Room

Frederick Road: Catonsville's "Main Street"

The Old Corner Store on the northwest corner of Frederick Road and Ingleside Avenue during this period served successively as the quarters of businesses operated by Joseph P. Fusting, John S. Wilson, Charles Fusting, and Marsden & Owens. In this photograph, circa 1898, it housed the latter establishment. Pictured, left to right, are the three Wysham brothers, Joshuah Marsden, and John Unger.
Elizabeth Peddicord

Frederick Road: Catonsville's "Main Street"

Advertisement in The Argus, *January 4, 1890.*

The Railroad Hotel, shown here circa 1900, was located across Frederick Road from the Short Line depot on the present site of the Catonsville Fire Station. Catonsville Room

Frederick Road: Catonsville's "Main Street"

This 1881 photo shows Albert Smith's office in the front of his residence at the southwest corner of Frederick Road and Bloomsbury Avenue. His steam mill, the first in the area to use stationary steam power, was located north of Frederick Road; it cut cordwood and ground mixed grain. To the right can be seen the door of the first office and shop of The Argus, *the community's recently established newspaper. The former Smith building currently houses the Shepherd's Place Bookstore.*
Catonsville Room

Hotel advertisements from The Argus, *June 17, 1899. The Catonsville Hotel was located near the southeast corner of Frederick Road and Bloomsbury Avenue. The Terminal Hotel sat at the end of the No. 8 streetcar line on Frederick Road.*

Frederick Road: Catonsville's "Main Street"

The Terminal Hotel, owned for many years by James Stoddard, was built at the western terminus of the Catonsville horsecar line. The Palm Garden in the rear was a popular establishment for local entertaining. The Terminal Hotel building has always served as a restaurant; currently it is the site of Russell's, Ltd., 1600 Frederick Road.
Jean Walsh

An article in *The Argus*, October 10, 1892, announced the Eden Terrace development:

Eden Terrace

The old Armitage property, which was purchased by the Eden Construction Company, is being transformed into beautiful building sites, and will be known as "Eden Terrace." Three avenues are being laid off, which will be known as Eastern, Western and Central avenues, which will intersect each other, the latter one leading to Edmondson Avenue. All will start from the Frederick road. This plan will present a fine effect, as the avenues and lots will be shaded with beautiful trees. The land is high and dry, and commands a fine view of the surrounding country. A unique feature of the terrace will be "Eden Lake," which will be formed in the eastern end, near Edmondson Avenue, and will be filled with pure sparkling water from the adjacent streams.

There will be 56 lots in the terrace, which average about 200 x 225 feet. The avenues will be forty feet wide, and all of the residences will set back fifty feet from their lines. The cost of the residences to be erected there will range from $3,500 to $12,000. Mr. Victor G. Bloede, the president of the company will erect a house for his own use to cost about $12,000. The company will probably erect fifteen houses at once, and offer them for sale on reasonable terms. A more beautiful and healthful location for a home cannot be found in the State than "Eden Terrace." It will be of easy access to the Short Line, Catonsville Railway and Edmondson Avenue Electric road. It affords an excellent field for both the home-seeker and investor, as lots there will steadily increase in value.

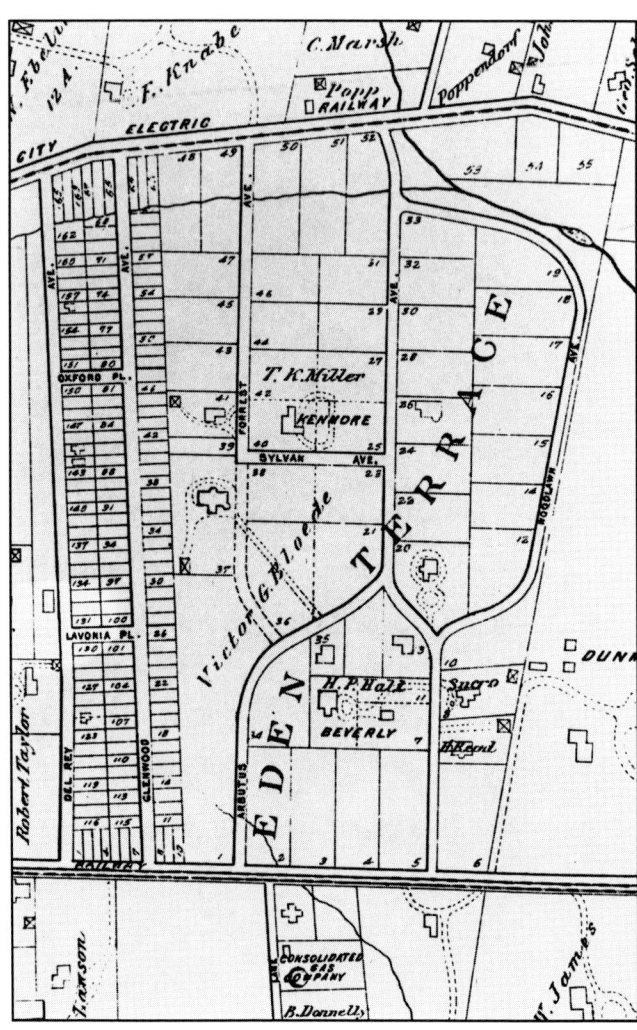

Detail of Eden Terrace from the Bromley Atlas *of 1898.*

Victorian Elegance: The Eden Terrace Subdivision

Arden, the home of Victor G. Bloede, was erected on land that his Eden Construction Company began to develop in the 1890s. Bloede's entrepreneurship also included the Caton Spring Company, the Patapsco Light Company, and the Edmondson Avenue, Catonsville & Ellicott City Electric Railway. Estimated to cost $13,000, Arden was the most lavish home in the exclusive subdivision. It burned in December, 1922.

A number of Eden Terrace homes were demolished in the 1950s to make way for the Baltimore Beltway.
Catonsville Room

Victorian Elegance: The Eden Terrace Subdivision

The first house built in Eden Terrace was a residence for the Sucro family at 13 Woodlawn Avenue, shown here in 1892. Pictured in front of their house was Mr. and Mrs. George C. Sucro (seated on settee at left); their son Fred Sucro (standing); daughter Jennie Sucro (with dark sash, sitting on the grass); daughter Antoinette Sucro (sitting low on slope); son William Sucro (sitting far right between dogs). Others in the photo are friends of the family. Two servants are on the porch. The house is still occupied by descendants of the Sucro family.
Antoinette Lawrence Hughes

Victorian Elegance: The Eden Terrace Subdivision

Around the turn of the century, the Fourth of July was celebrated on the lawn at Gray Gables, the home of Charles Wacker, on Arbutus Avenue in Eden Terrace. Pictured left to right, are Carl Schon, Willy Sucro, George Schon, unidentified, Carl Bloede, and Will Forster. Jacques Kelly

Victorian Elegance: The Eden Terrace Subdivision

The Eden Terrace home of H. P. Hall was built at a cost of $8,000. The photograph is from the late 1890s.
Catonsville Room

Victorian Elegance: The Eden Terrace Subdivision

*House at 101 Arbutus Avenue in Eden Terrace, circa 1898.
Catonsville Room*

Victorian Elegance: The Eden Terrace Subdivision

The Bloede carriage, with members of the Bloede and Wacker families, sits in front of the Brink house, Eden Terrace. The house was built circa 1898 for Charles Brink, president of a Baltimore storage company.
Jacques Kelly

Victorian Elegance: The Eden Terrace Subdivision

Dorothy Forster Wacker, Elsie Bion, and an unidentified gentleman play tennis at Gray Gables in 1913.
Jacques Kelly

Carla, Ilse, Olga, and Dorothy Wacker pose at Gray Gables at an unknown time.
Jacques Kelly

Social Life in the 1880s and 1890s

Tennis match at the Catonsville Casino, an early country club, which provided a social center for the elite families of the region. Shown here around 1905, the structure was built in the 1890s and destroyed by fire in 1906. A new facility was erected in 1908 and renamed the Catonsville Country Club. In the 1920s, the property was sold to the Baltimore County School Board for the new Catonsville High School.
Jacques Kelly

Mrs. Harriet (Jones) Smith stands by George Jerome Smith on a tricycle, in the late nineteenth century.
Dorothy Maisel Reis

Social Life in the 1880s and 1890s

Edith, Florence, and Julia Jones are joined by two guests from Pennsylvania on the porch steps of the family home at 10 Newburg Avenue. Julia Jones was a local schoolteacher, Florence the village postmistress, and Edith the housekeeper.
Dorothy Maisel Reis

Social Life in the 1880s and 1890s

The Catonsville School, sixth and seventh grade classes, are shown about 1881. Mr. Comegys, the principal, is near the center with mustache.
Catonsville Room

Social Life in the 1880s and 1890s

Unidentified tennis players enjoy a game.
Dorothy Maisel Reis

A croquet game is played by unidentified young ladies in Catonsville in the late decades of the nineteenth century.
Dorothy Maisel Reis

Social Life in the 1880s and 1890s

St. Timothy's Episcopal Church Sunday School children gather with their teachers in the late nineteenth century.
Catonsville Room

Social Life in the 1880s and 1890s

Dorothy, Olga, and baby Ilse Wacker play in the yard at Brink House, Eden Terrace, date unknown.

An Estate Family: The Lurmans

This portrait of Gustav W. Lurman, Jr., was painted in 1896. During the Civil War, Lurman, like a number of other Baltimore County residents, fought for the Confederacy; at the time he was a teenager.
Catonsville Room

An Estate Family: The Lurmans

Theodor Lurman, Gustav Jr.'s younger brother, is pictured here in 1886 in one of the family's many surreys. Theodor also inherited a portion of the Farmlands estate from their father. In 1880, as a young man of thirty, he still lived with his mother on the estate, according to the census of that year.
Catonsville Room

The family of Gustav W. Lurman, Jr., appeared in the 1880 U.S. manuscript census. Gustav, Jr., inherited a large portion of the Farmlands estate when his father, Gustav W. Lurman, Sr., died in 1866. The elder Lurman's fortune came from commercial activities in Baltimore. The younger Lurman, a person of considerable wealth, is listed in the census as a "farmer." The census also records his wife, Elizabeth, and their three children: E. Deb. (Elizabeth), age thirteen; F. D. (Frances), age ten; and K. (Katharine), age six.

An Estate Family: The Lurmans

Gustav Lurman, Jr., and his daughter, Frances, on the porch of their home, 1892. In 1881 Lurman had constructed a new estate home, Bloomsbury, for his family. Catonsville Room

An Estate Family: The Lurmans

An avid horsewoman, Frances won trophies in both cross-country riding and hunting. Here she stands with one of her horses at Farmlands, circa 1900. Frances sold the Farmlands estate in 1948 and died in 1950.
Catonsville Room

Frances D. Lurman, the most well-known daughter of Gustav and Elizabeth, was regarded as one of Baltimore's most beautiful women. She remained single until 1947, when—in her 70s—she married Dorsey W. Williams, a man she had first met when she was a teenager.
Catonsville Room

An Estate Family: The Lurmans

The Victorian elegance of the parlor at Farmlands was photographed circa 1900. Farmlands was the name Gustav W. Lurman, Sr., gave the six hundred-acre estate he purchased in 1848. The house itself, built by Hammond Dorsey, dated to approximately 1820.
Catonsville Room

An Estate Family: The Lurmans

An Estate Family: The Lurmans

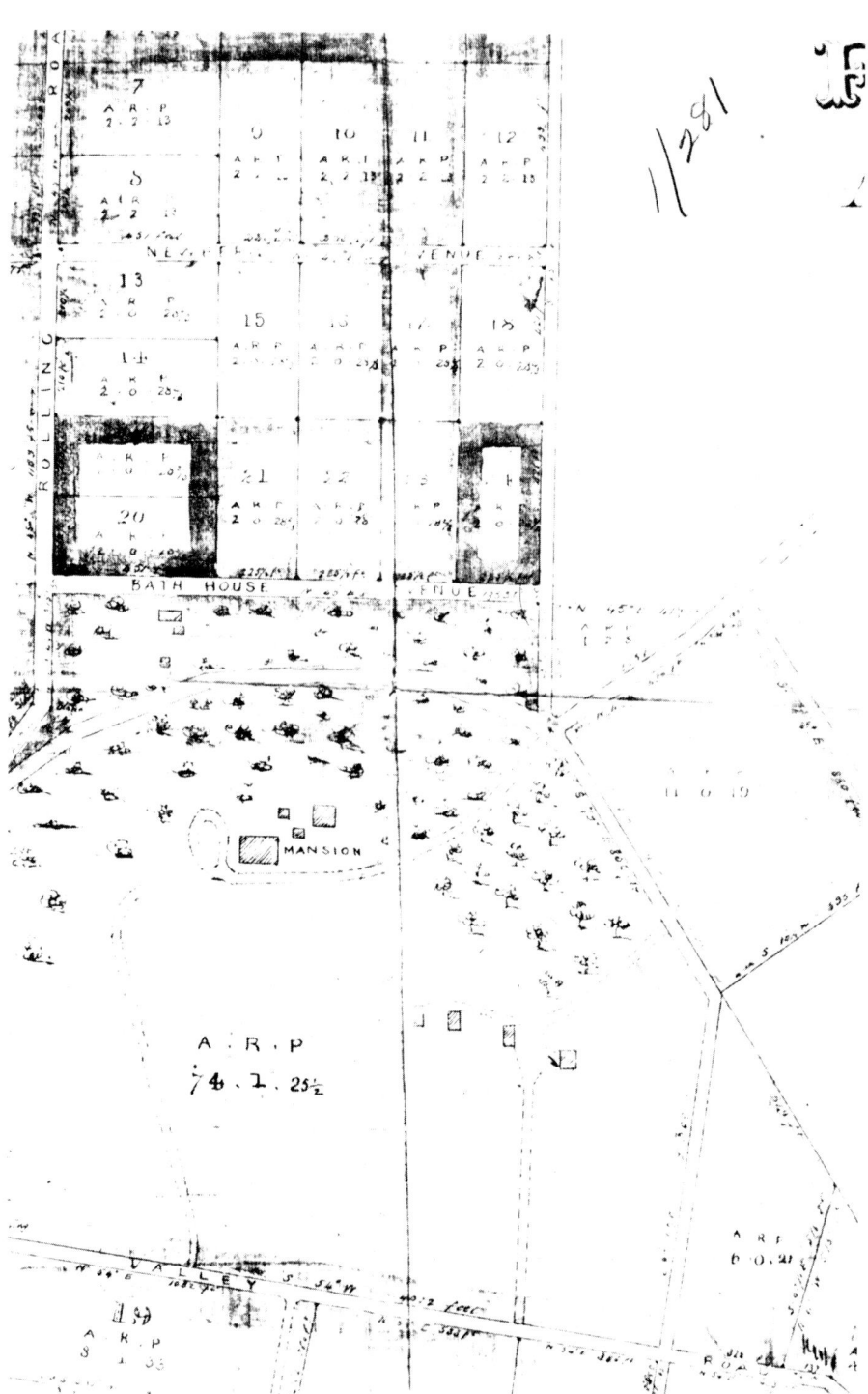

Detail from a surveyor's map of Farmlands, was executed in 1879 for Frances Donnell Lurman, widow of Gustav, Sr., apparently to show how the estate would be laid out in lots for distribution to her children. Note the lot numbers on the map; a section of the map (not shown) listed the lot number allocations. Mrs. Lurman died in 1885.

Shown here are the Farmlands mansion house and lots on the northern portion of the estate, which Mrs. Lurman retained for herself. The map indicated the assignment of the large portion south of Valley Road (visible at the bottom of this detail) to Gustav, Jr., who built Bloomsbury there. South of Wilkens (not pictured here) was a large tract assigned to Theodor. Others receiving assignments were son John and daughters Josephine, Franny, and Minna.

Note Rolling Road on the west, Newburg across the top, the undesignated road following roughly the route of the present Bloomsbury Avenue (between the mansion and "Bath House Avenue"), and Valley Road at the bottom.
Catonsville Room

An Estate Family: The Lurmans

*Farmlands, circa 1910. The stuccoed brick house contained nine bedrooms, four bathrooms, and fourteen other large rooms. In 1948, Frances Lurman sold the estate to the Baltimore County Department of Education; in 1953 the new Catonsville Senior High School opened on the former site of the mansion house.
Catonsville Room*

*In the gardens at Farmlands, Gustav W. Lurman, Sr., reputedly laid out the estate's spacious grounds and planted rare specimens of trees and shrubbery. The grounds included an English flower garden, the greenhouse, and a grapery. When the estate was acquired as the site for the new high school, the deed included provisions for the care and maintenance of trees and shrubbery on the grounds, as well as a clause permitting the family of the caretaker and the family's male heirs to continue to reside in the stone cottage in perpetuity.
Catonsville Room*

*Bloomsbury, built by Gustav, Jr., in 1881. In 1916 it was acquired as part of the property for the new Rolling Road Golf Club; it is one of the earliest clubhouse structures in continuous use, but in 1989 was scheduled for possible demolition.
Catonsville Room*

Early electrified streetcars on the No. 8 line could be converted to have open sides during the summer. The line's route, first established in the 1860s for horsecars, extended from Catonsville down Frederick Road to Baltimore, then out York Road to Towson, linking the city with these two growing suburban areas. Baltimore Streetcar Museum Collection

Chapter IV

Streetcar Suburb, 1900 to 1920

Double tracks down the center of Frederick Road and tall overhead electric lines dominated the village streetscape by the beginning of the new century. Catonsville had become a bustling suburban community.

New structures along Frederick were symptomatic of changing times. At Frederick and Ingleside the Romanesque arches and impressive stonework of the new building of the First National Bank of Catonsville, opened in 1902, conveyed a sense of security and financial stability for the five-year-old institution. Across the street, the new Catonsville High School, completed in 1910, accommodated the community's growing (white) youth population. At the opposite end of the village, significant new construction occurred in 1903 at Frederick Road and Newburg Avenue when the frame building housing *The Argus* was moved back and the durable stone walls of the Masonic Temple and Salem Lutheran Church were erected across the street from one another. The congregation's relocation brought this German-descended institution to the heart of the village from its earlier location on Ingleside Avenue. When the congregation simultaneously dropped German for English as the language of its worship services, ethnicity was joining the mainstream.

In the residential part of town, the focus of this period increasingly was upon the development of permanent housing rather than seasonal occupancy. Catering to a somewhat affluent constituency were Oak Forest Park, Forest Spring Park, and Ten Hills. Typical of the appeal such developments evoked was the designation of the

Streetcar Suburb, 1900 to 1920

latter as "the country suburb."

Catonsville's continuing growth brought two important political challenges. In the 1880s and again in the early 1900s a small but vocal group of Catonsville's residents pushed for legal incorporation, but each time the majority of local voters rejected it decisively. At the same time, Baltimore City political leaders sought to bring Catonsville and other portions of Baltimore County within the orbit of the municipality with various proposals for annexation during the second decade of the new century. Baltimore's annexation of county areas in 1918 spared most of Catonsville, but brought the city boundary to approximately a mile from the village center.

Reconsideration of women's traditional roles was part of the social and political history of Catonsville during these decades. Clearly, there was uneasiness over this issue. Some women played an active part in the movement for female suffrage, although *The Argus* scoffed at a group of "several suffrage advocates" who had "invaded" the village "in a large automobile" in 1910, distributing pro-suffrage literature. Nevertheless, women became an increasingly important element in the public affairs of the local community. The Women's Civic League, formed in 1911, sought to secure "clean air, clean streets, clean milk and better conditions generally" in the village of Catonsville.

While gender relations began to change in the village, traditional patterns of race relations persisted relatively unaltered. This factor was evident in 1907 when the proposal for a new white school led to considerable opposition to the use of the old school (originally built in 1878) for Catonsville's black children. Some opponents expressed the view that it would bring them too close to the town center. The issue finally was resolved to the satisfaction of the white community when the decision was made to sell the old brick school building to St. Mark parish as a parochial school. Blacks continued to attend the Colored School at Edmondson Avenue and Winters Lane (then on the northern edge of the town center) in a small building with no electricity and only a stove for heat.

The prosperity of Catonsville—and the nation—in the years from 1900 to 1917 meant that an increasing number of families could afford new housing. As a result, Catonsville began to spread out from its Frederick Road axis. Large frame houses with spacious yards were built on wide avenues while small bungalows and cottages, with modest little yards, were erected on narrower streets. Even some of the families in the Winters Lane black community, constrained for the most part to low-paying service jobs, were able to save enough to build attractive new houses.

World War I abruptly brought new building to a halt. However, in 1918 Catonsville was poised for the unprecedented boom years of the 1920s. Gone were the notices of the summer home openings, replaced with articles announcing the subdivision of former estates. By the late 'teens a new civic concern increasingly found voice in *The Argus:* the auto. Even more than the streetcar, it would become the agent of dramatic change.

A Page from the 1910 Manuscript Census

Starting in 1790, the United States government has conducted a census every ten years. At first simply a head count, successive censuses have been expanded to collect more and more information from the nation's inhabitants.

The actual handwritten forms filled out by census takers as they walked the streets and interviewed residents are called the manuscript census. The original documents are preserved at the National Archives in Washington, D.C. Copies are readily available to the public in microfilm form at many libraries. The Albin O. Kuhn Library at UMBC and Baltimore's Enoch Pratt Free Library, Central Branch, have on microfilm all the available records for Maryland through the 1910 census.

For reasons of privacy and confidentiality the manuscript version of the census, with its record of information by name, is not released for seventy-two years; therefore, the 1910 manuscript census is the most recent available.

The statistical totals on the following pages were compiled by UMBC student participants in the Catonsville History Project: Ken Arrington, Marc Berman, Suzanne Gasser, Mary Gerstenberger, Kelly Grace Gilberto, Patrick McGregor, and Linda Rayman.

The copy of the manuscript census page is page 2B for the First Precinct of the First District of Baltimore County. Note that "Catonsville Village" had been written, then crossed out. This page was completed by local census enumerator John Peregoy on April 18, 1910 whose signature is in the upper right hand corner.

Recorded here is information on those residing in household addresses 11 through 21 on Newburg Avenue and 34 through 38 on Sanford Avenue. The columns include detailed information on each individual resident. National Archives

A Page from the 1910 Manuscript Census

General tabulations from the manuscript census ledgers are published in the U.S. census reports soon after each decennial census is completed. Aggregate figures are listed for the national, state, and local level. Published volumes of the U.S. census reports can be found in most area libraries.

Above is a page from the population tables for the state of Maryland. It lists the total population figures for Baltimore County by district; the First District was comprised of Catonsville and its surrounding countryside.
Thirteenth census of the United States, Population, 1910, Vol. II (1913)

Sanborn Fire Insurance Atlas of Catonsville, 1910

Maps for most cities and towns in the United States were prepared by the Sanborn Map Company of New York City to aid firms insuring residential and commercial properties. They were revised and updated periodically.

The maps used color coding to specify the building materials of structures, an important consideration for fire insurance purposes. On these maps, wood is denoted by yellow, brick by red, and stone (or concrete) by blue.

Sanborn fire insurance maps are available in their original form at the Library of Congress, Map Division, and the McKeldin Library, University of Maryland College Park; they are available on microfilm at the Albin O. Kuhn Library, University of Maryland Baltimore County. The Catonsville Area Branch of the Baltimore County Public Library has the Sanborn map for 1930. These maps are from the McKeldin Library, University of Maryland College Park.

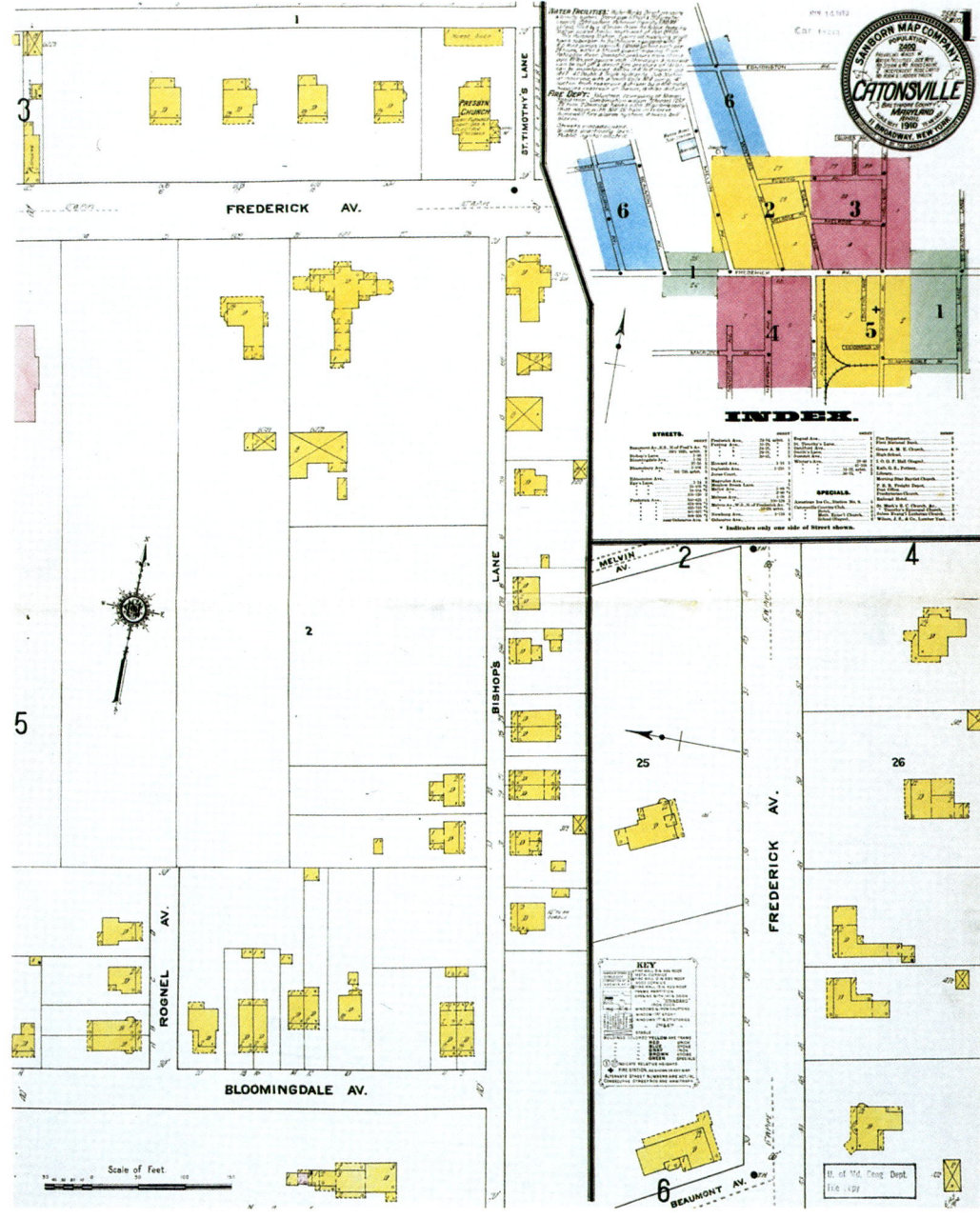

Sanborn Fire Insurance Atlas of Catonsville, 1910

Sanborn Fire Insurance Atlas of Catonsville, 1910

Sanborn Fire Insurance Atlas of Catonsville, 1910

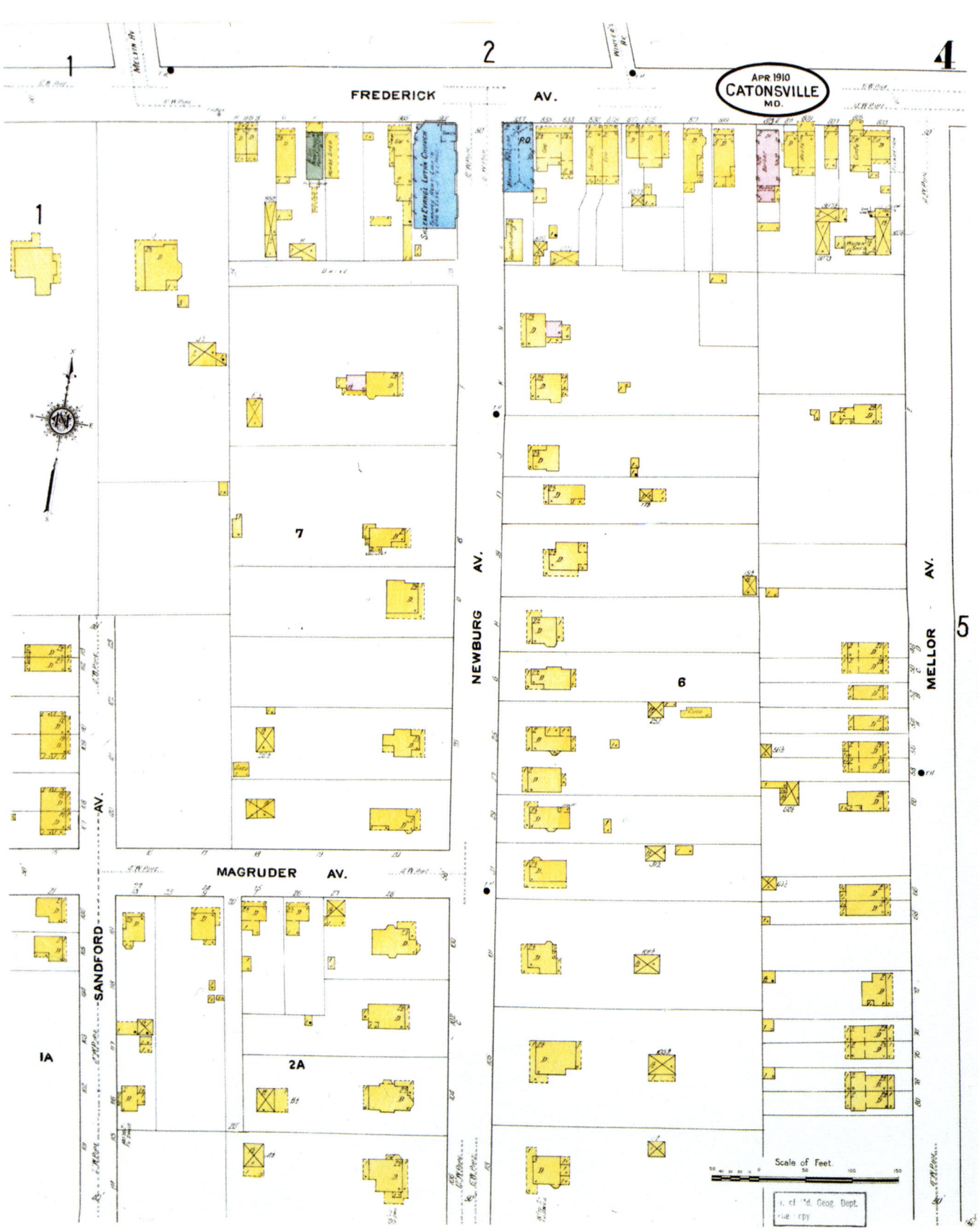

Sanborn Fire Insurance Atlas of Catonsville, 1910

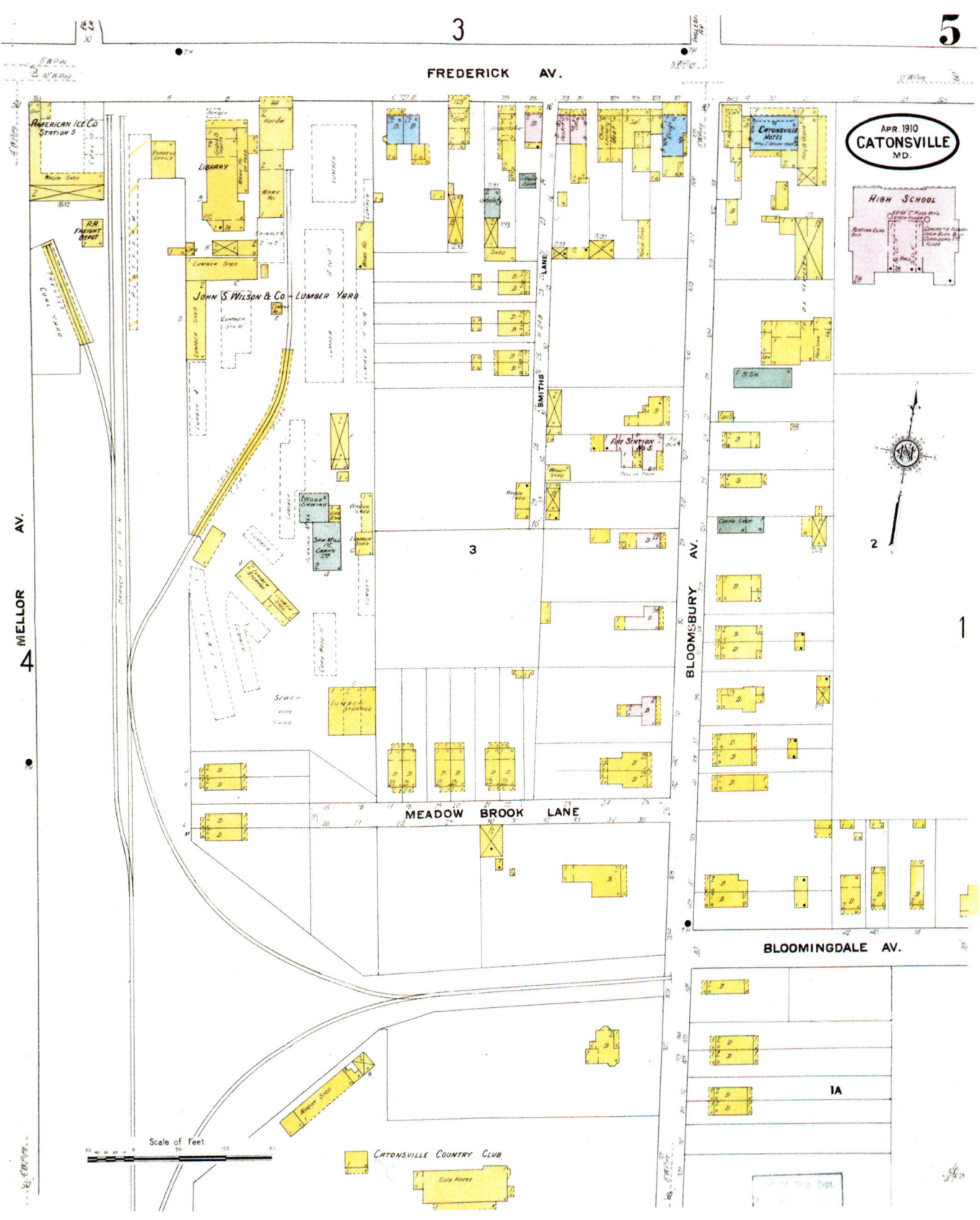

Sanborn Fire Insurance Atlas of Catonsville, 1910

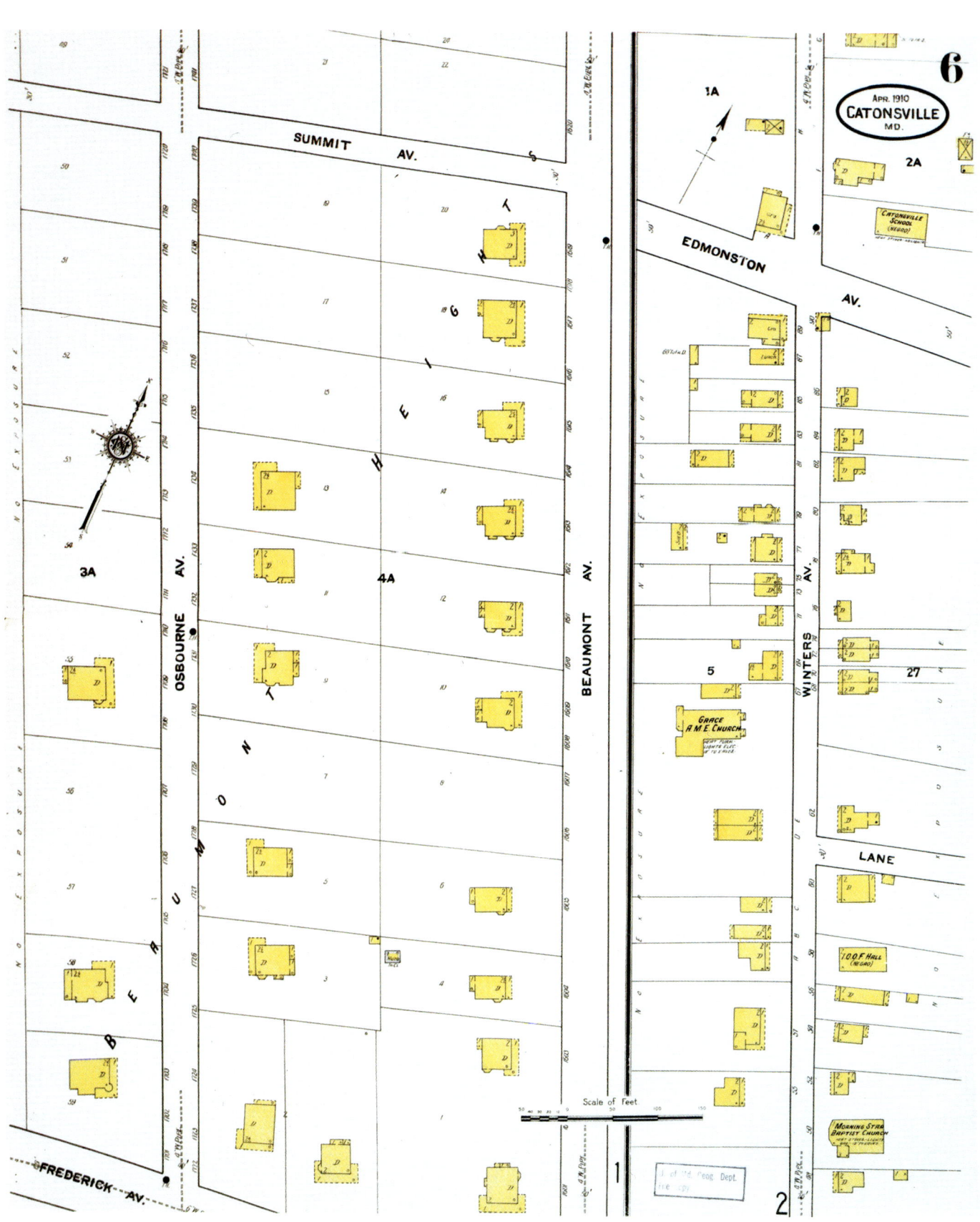

Mapping the 1910 Population

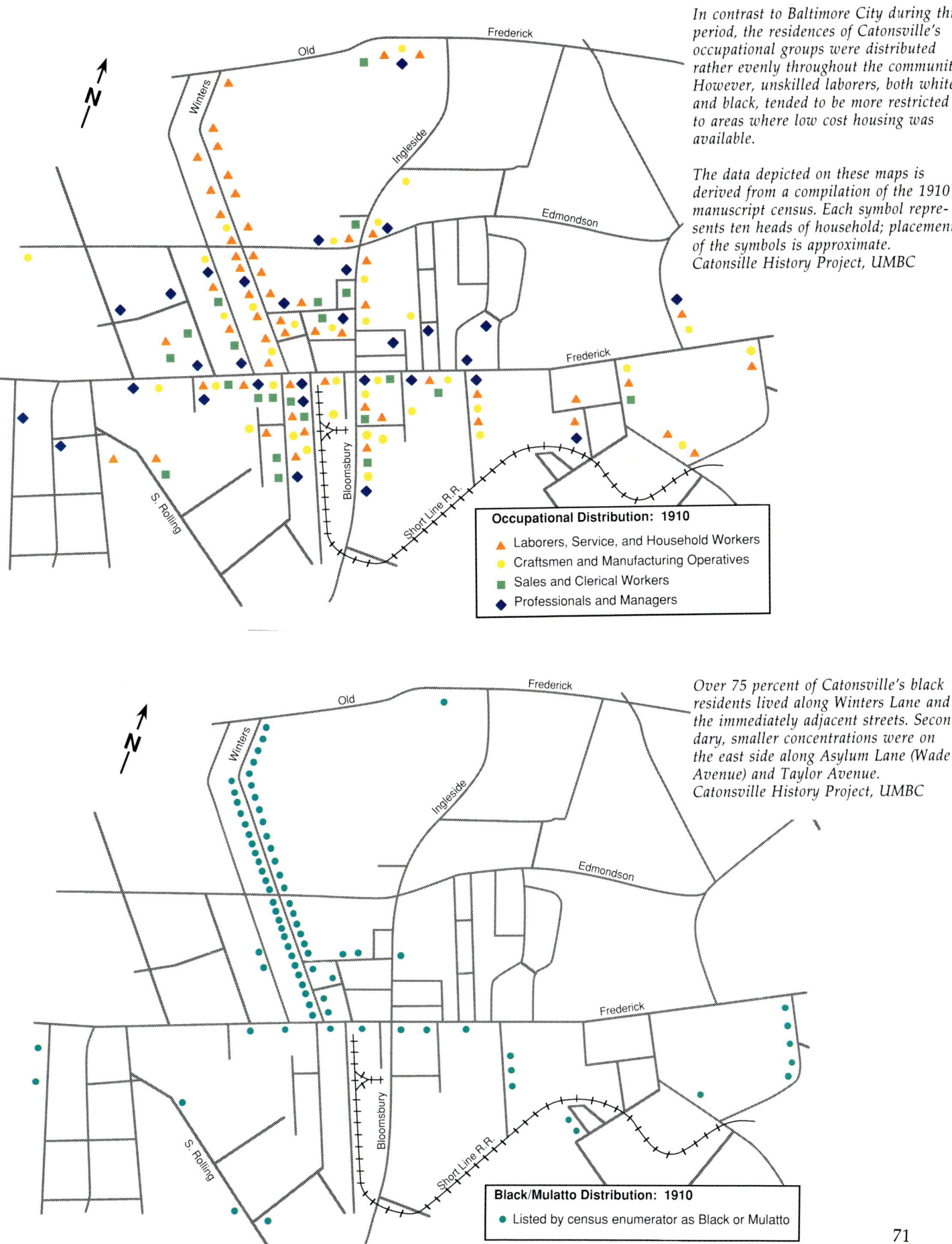

In contrast to Baltimore City during this period, the residences of Catonsville's occupational groups were distributed rather evenly throughout the community. However, unskilled laborers, both white and black, tended to be more restricted to areas where low cost housing was available.

The data depicted on these maps is derived from a compilation of the 1910 manuscript census. Each symbol represents ten heads of household; placement of the symbols is approximate.
Catonsville History Project, UMBC

Occupational Distribution: 1910
- ▲ Laborers, Service, and Household Workers
- ● Craftsmen and Manufacturing Operatives
- ■ Sales and Clerical Workers
- ◆ Professionals and Managers

Over 75 percent of Catonsville's black residents lived along Winters Lane and the immediately adjacent streets. Secondary, smaller concentrations were on the east side along Asylum Lane (Wade Avenue) and Taylor Avenue.
Catonsville History Project, UMBC

Black/Mulatto Distribution: 1910
- ● Listed by census enumerator as Black or Mulatto

Mapping the 1910 Population

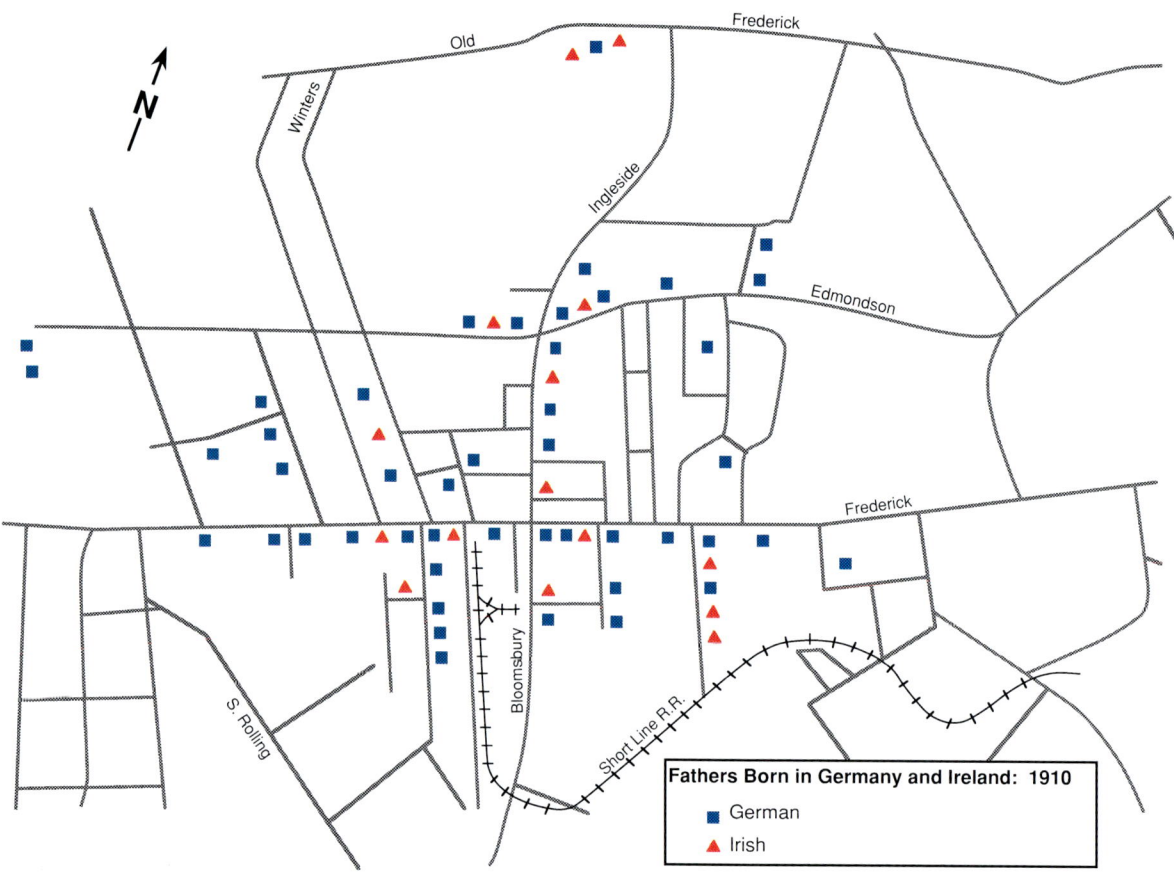

There were few clearly defined areas of ethnic concentration in Catonsville in 1910. Second generation German and Irish families, the only two foreign background groups of significant size, were distributed in a dispersed pattern similar to occupational groups. Germans were somewhat more concentrated on the north side along Ingleside; a small Irish-American cluster was evident along Asylum Lane.
Catonsville History Project, UMBC

Sanborn Fire Insurance Atlas of Catonsville, 1925

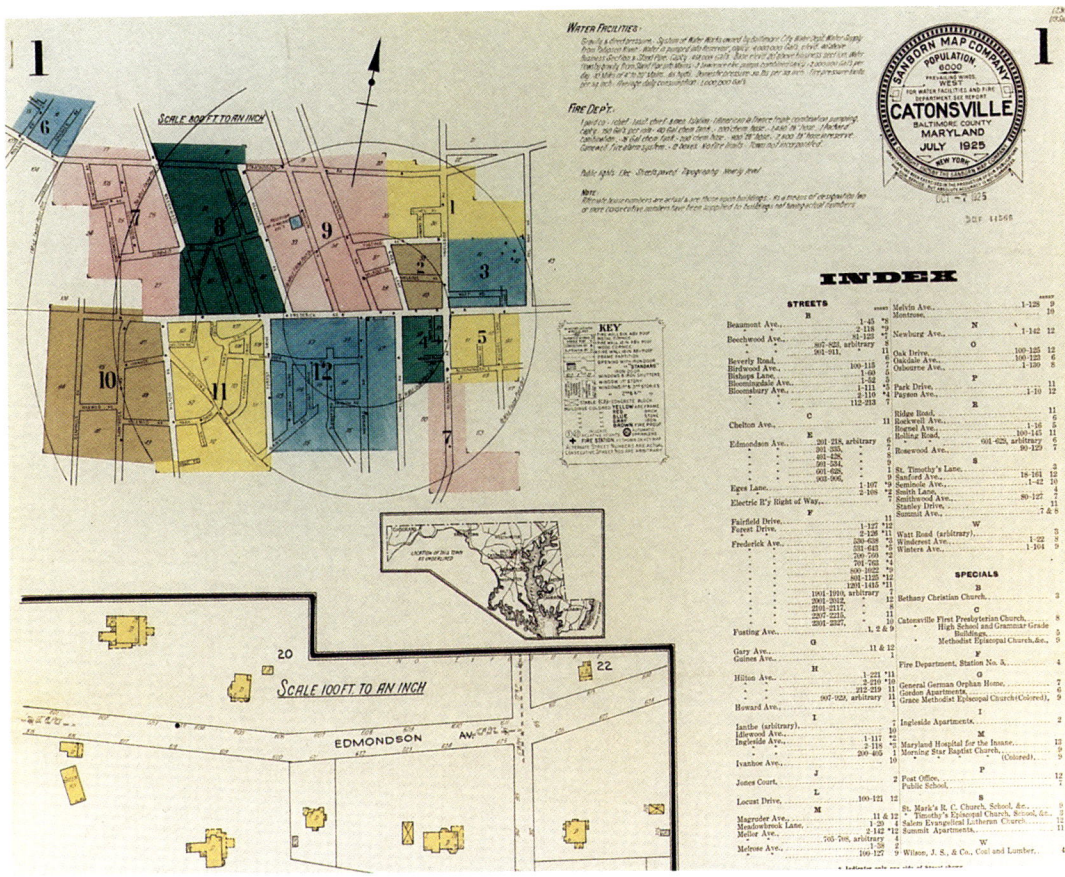

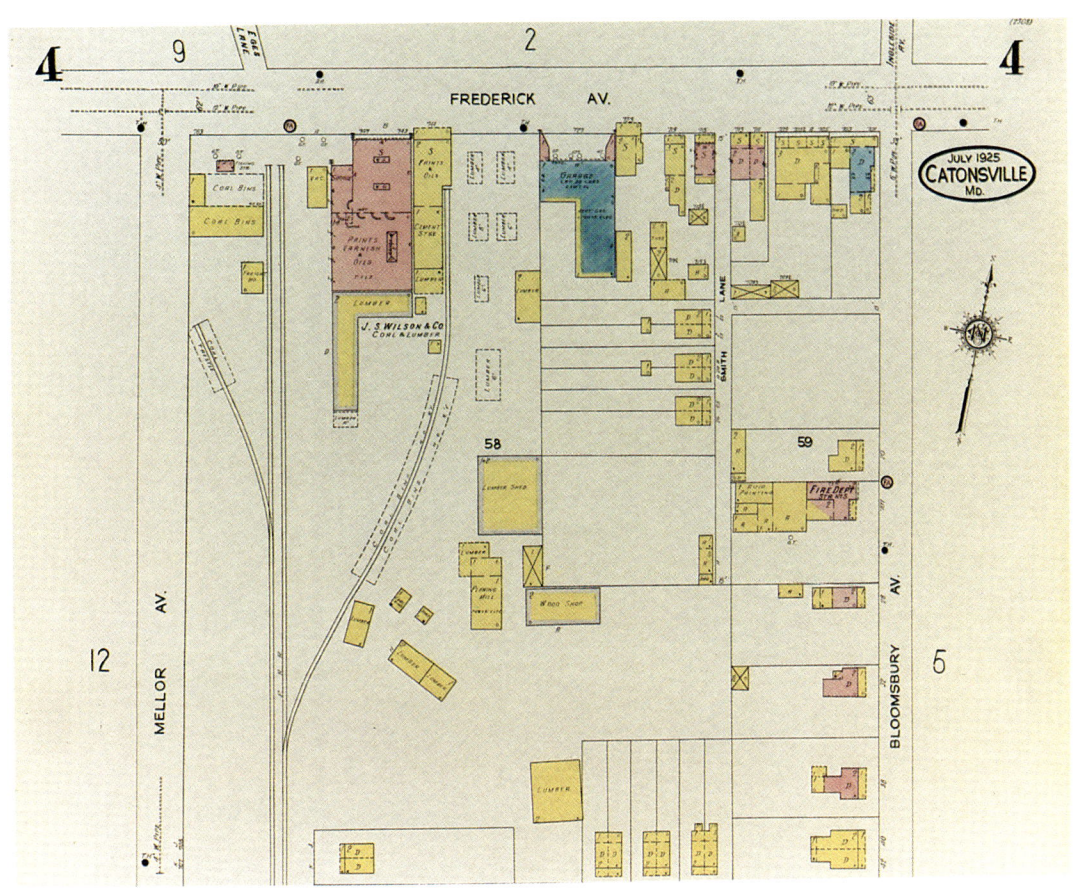

Sanborn Fire Insurance Atlas of Catonsville, 1925

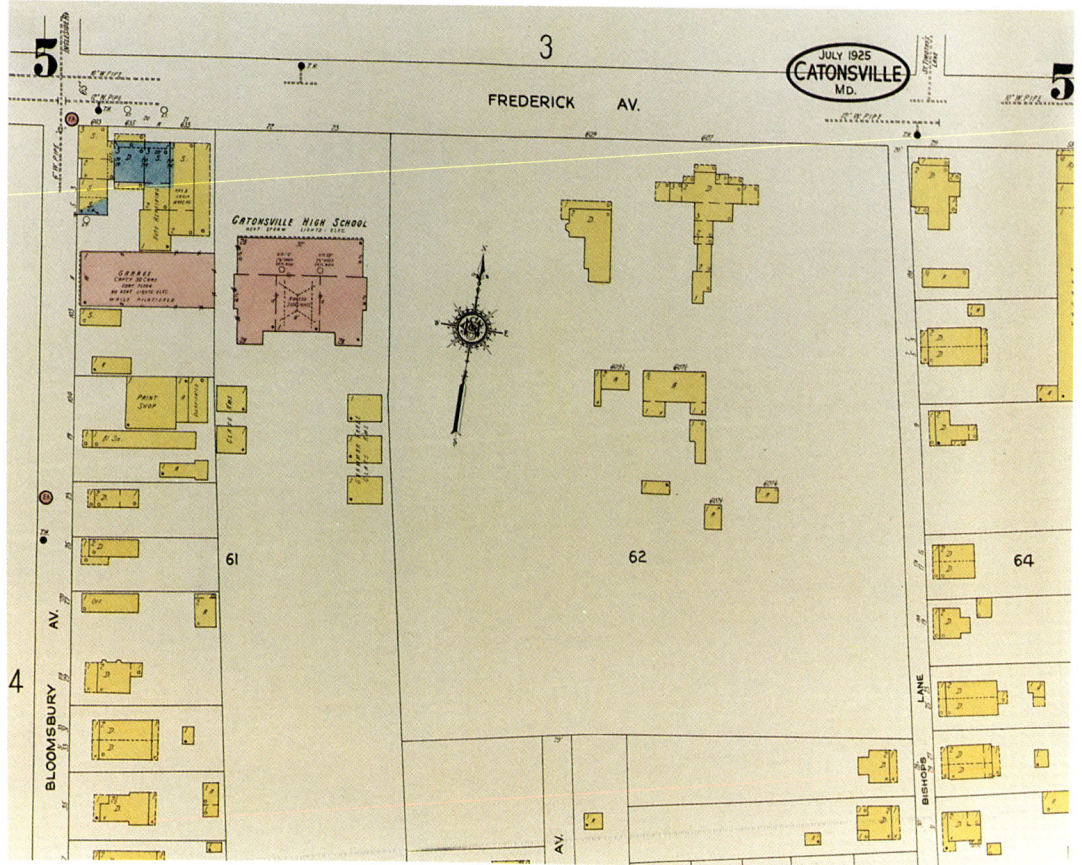

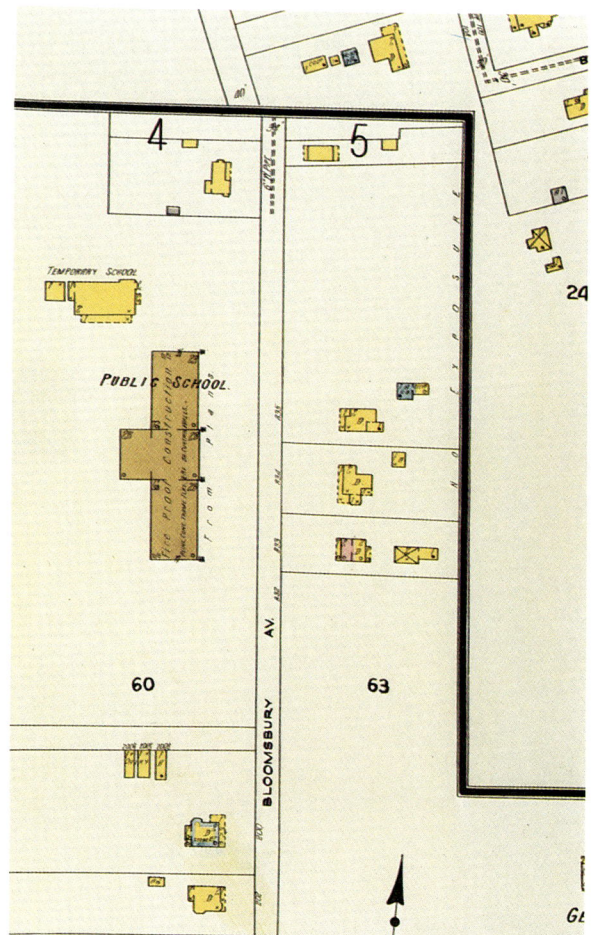

Sanborn Fire Insurance Atlas of Catonsville, 1925

75

Sanborn Fire Insurance Atlas of Catonsville, 1930

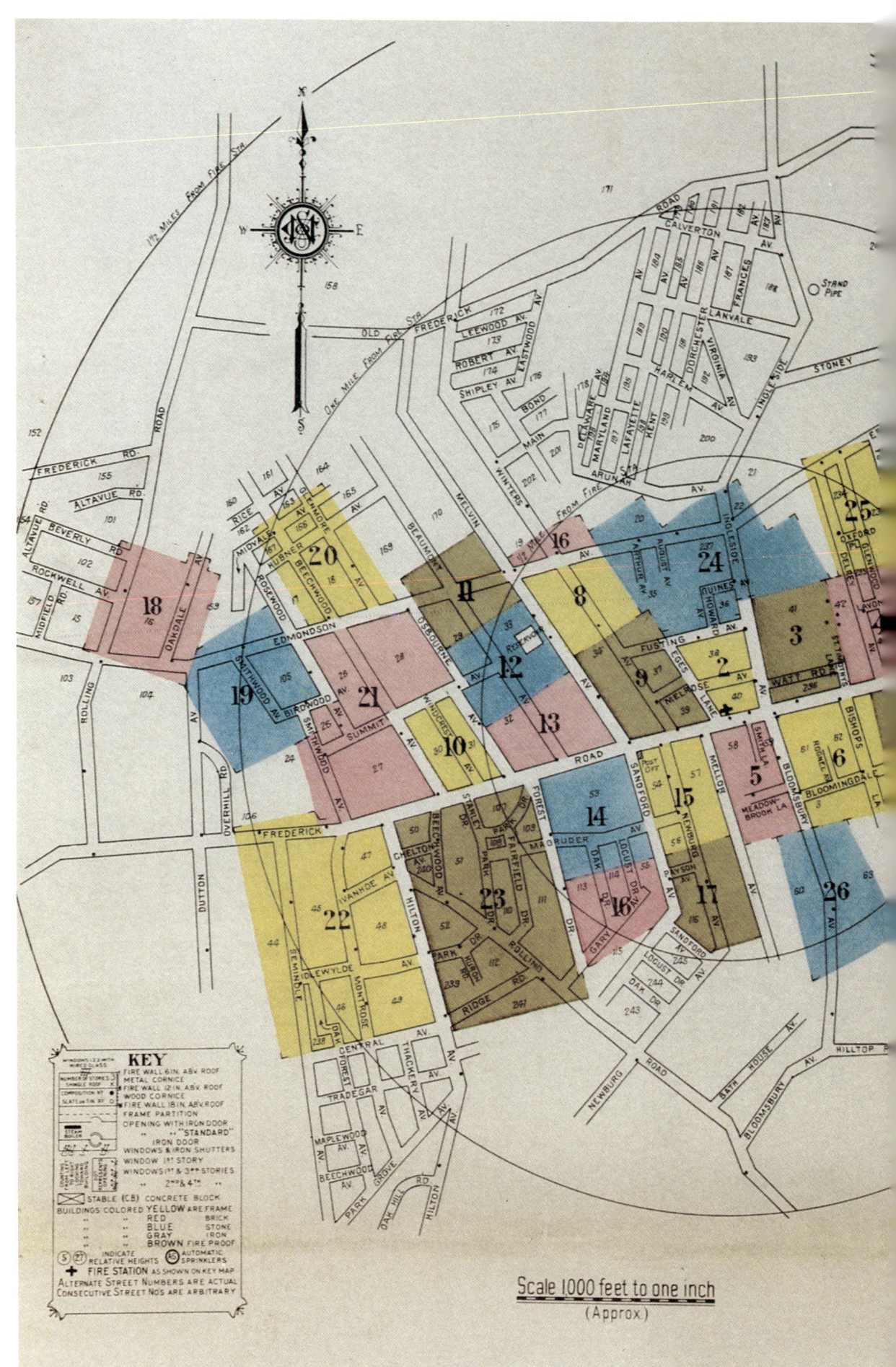

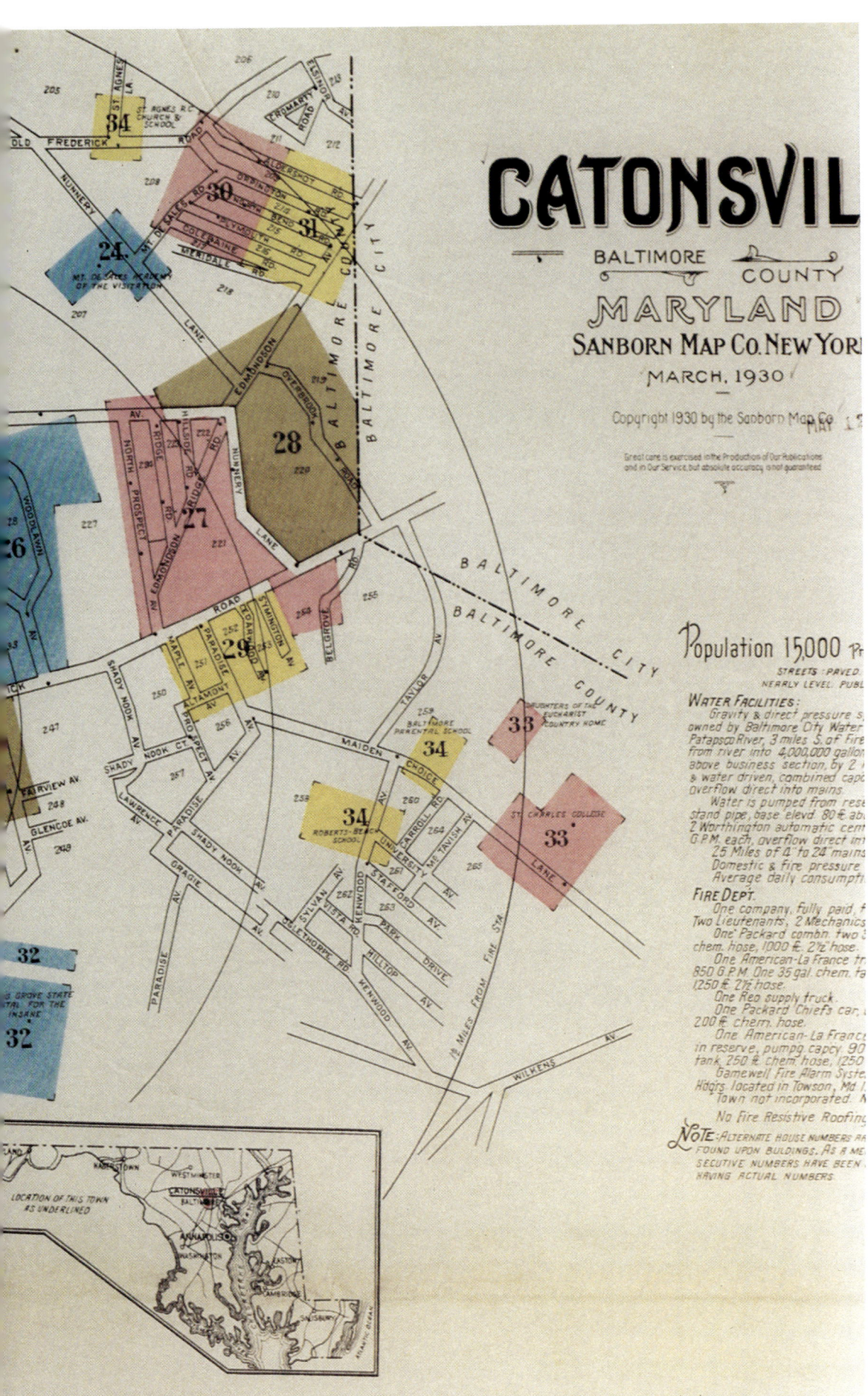

Sanborn Fire Insurance Atlas of Catonsville, 1930

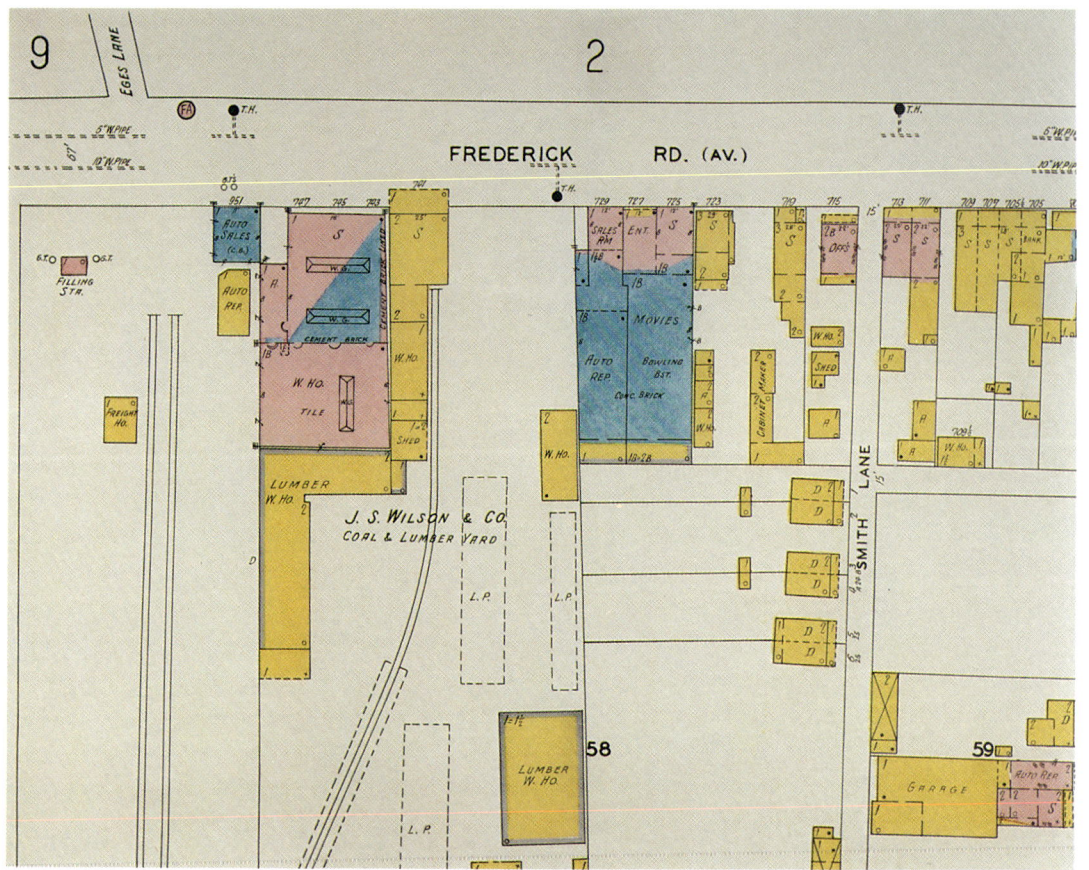

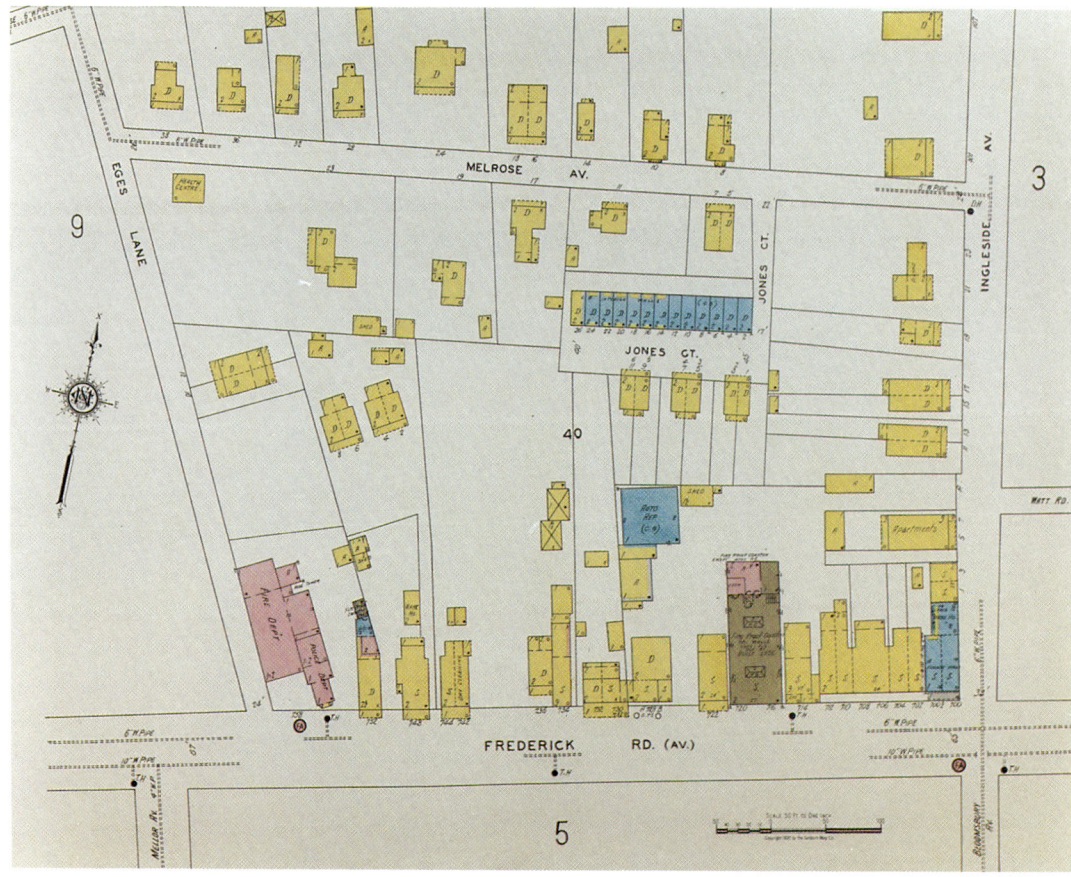

Sanborn Fire Insurance Atlas of Catonsville, 1930

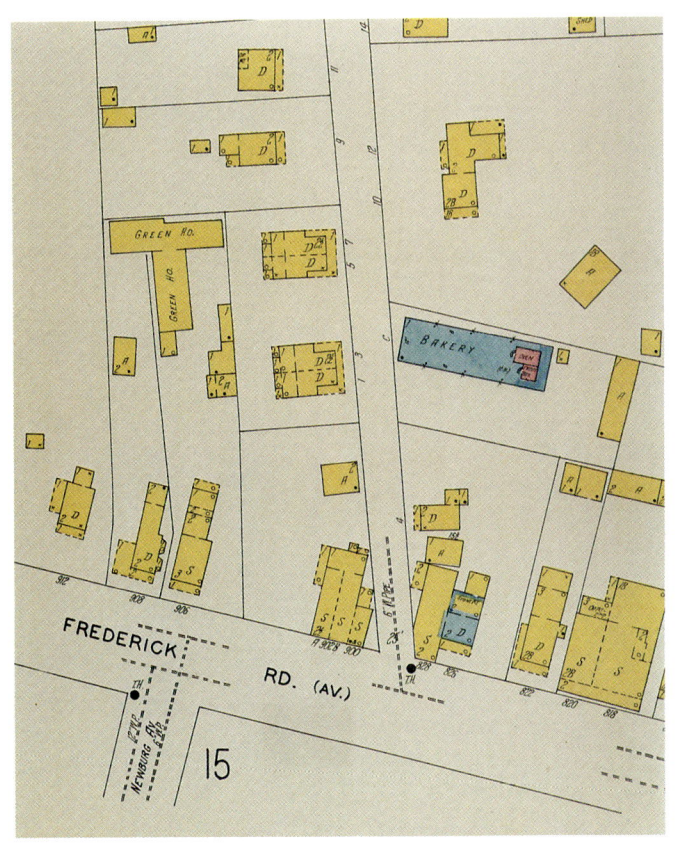
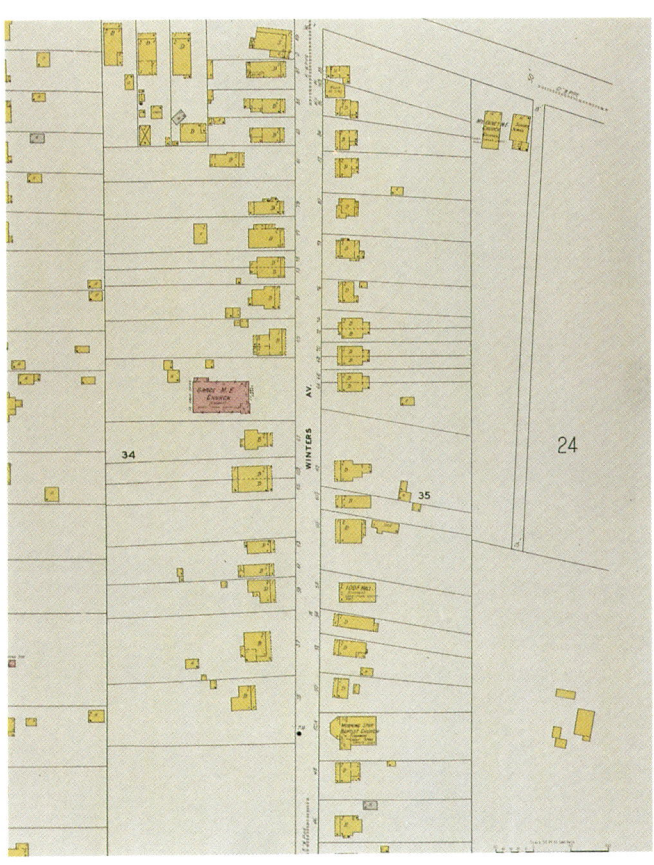

Sanborn Fire Insurance Atlas of Catonsville, 1930

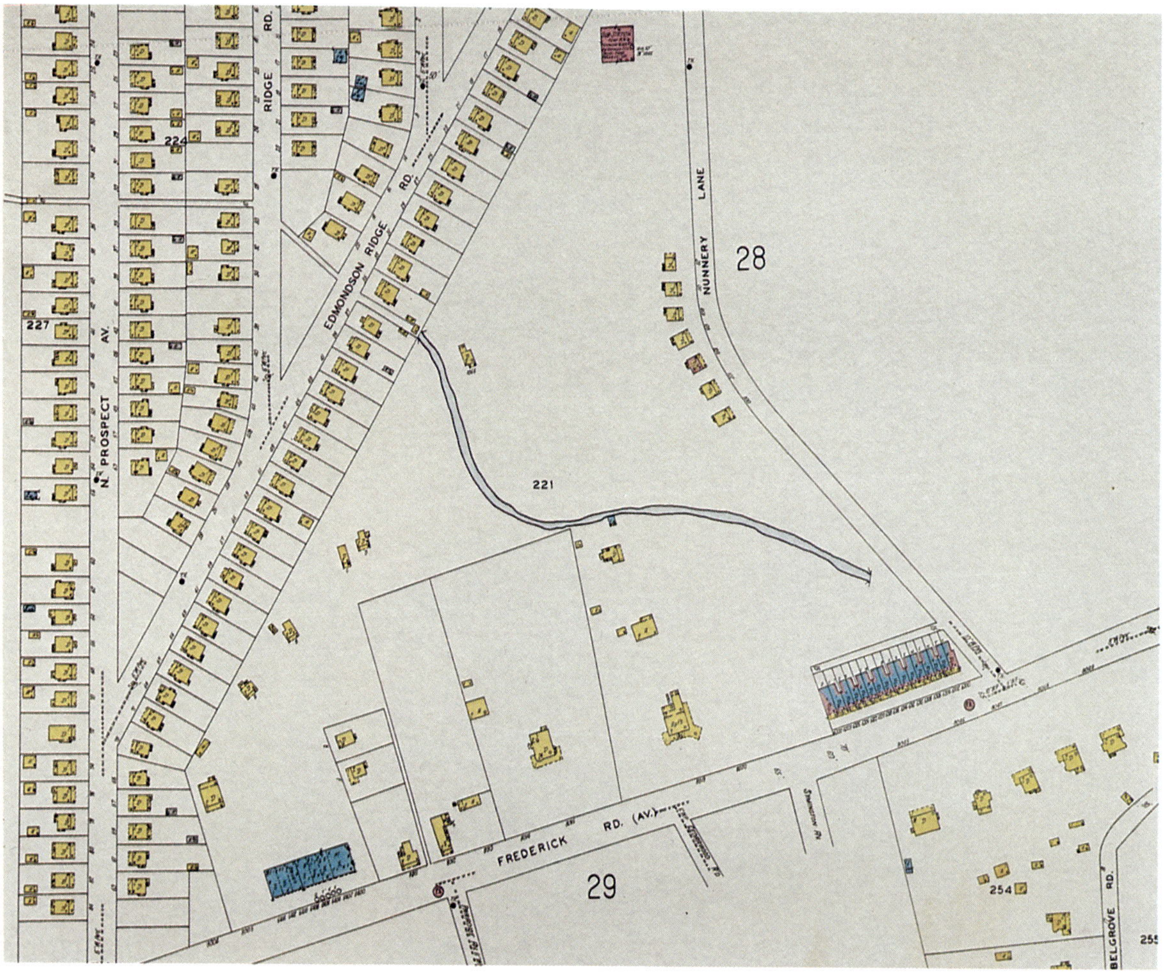

The 1910 Census: Work

The occupational section of the manuscript census ledger contained information on each person's trade and the nature of the work. For example, selected combinations from this page included, "Commission; Brokerage"; "Wholesale; Coffee House"; "Blacksmith; Wagons and Shoes"; "School; Teacher"; and "Cook; Private Family." In column 20, Emp=Employer; W=Employee; and OA=Own Account (note that the line listing "Wholesale; Coffee House" shows "OA" written over as a "W"; corrections of this kind show up frequently on the sheets).

The 1910 Census: Work

John Peregoy, seated in his grocery store, about 1920. Appointed as a census enumerator for the federal census of 1910, Peregoy canvassed the portion of Catonsville west of Ingleside and Bloomsbury, which comprised Baltimore County's Enumeration District Two for federal census purposes in that year. Catonsville Room

The 1910 Census: Work

Catonsville's white males were relatively evenly distributed across the spectrum of the major occupational categories. As in 1880, leading areas continued to be craftsmen (skilled trades) and managers (entrepreneurs and supervisors). However, such white-collar occupations as professionals, salesmen, and clerical workers counted significant numbers. Among traditional blue-collar occupations, common laborers ranked second to craftsmen; farm work continued to occupy only a small portion.

For black men, common laboring occupations predominated as they had in 1880, and there was a noticeable decline of farm work as a significant employer of blacks as well as whites.
Catonsville History Project, UMBC

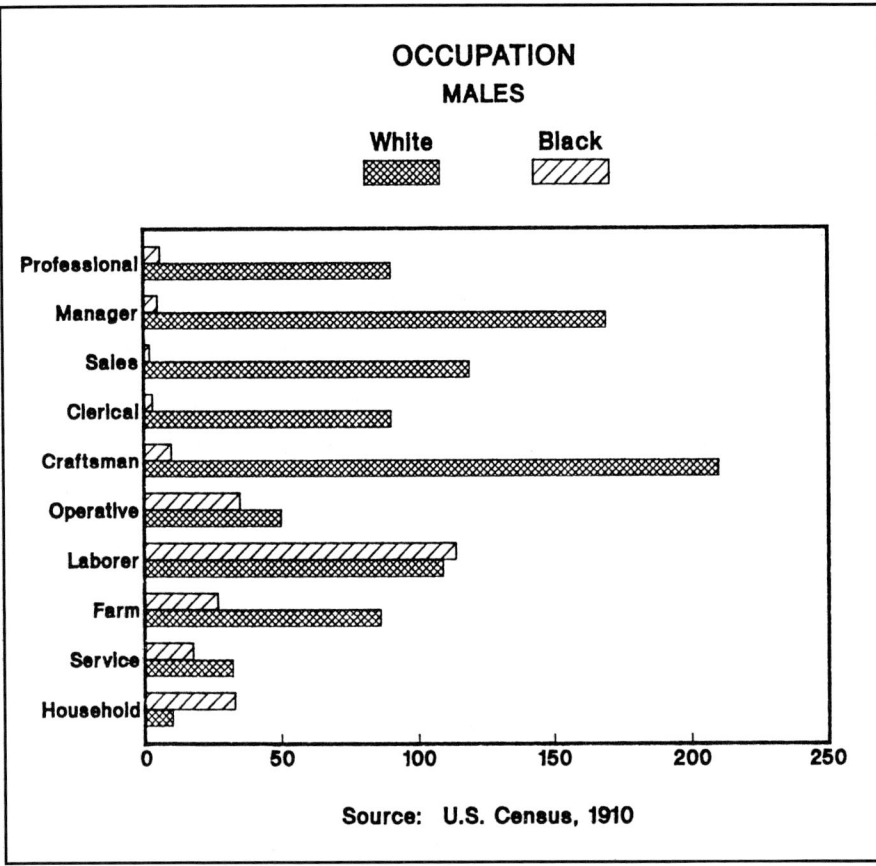

The experience of white and black women was quite different when it came to employment outside the home.
A relatively small proportion of white women were engaged in the paid labor force. Some were scattered in the white-collar areas as professionals, managers, sales, and clerical workers, but slightly more were in blue-collar work as manufacturing operatives or household (domestic servant) workers.

In contrast, more than two hundred black women were employed as household workers, and other options appeared to be quite limited.
Catonsville History Project, UMBC

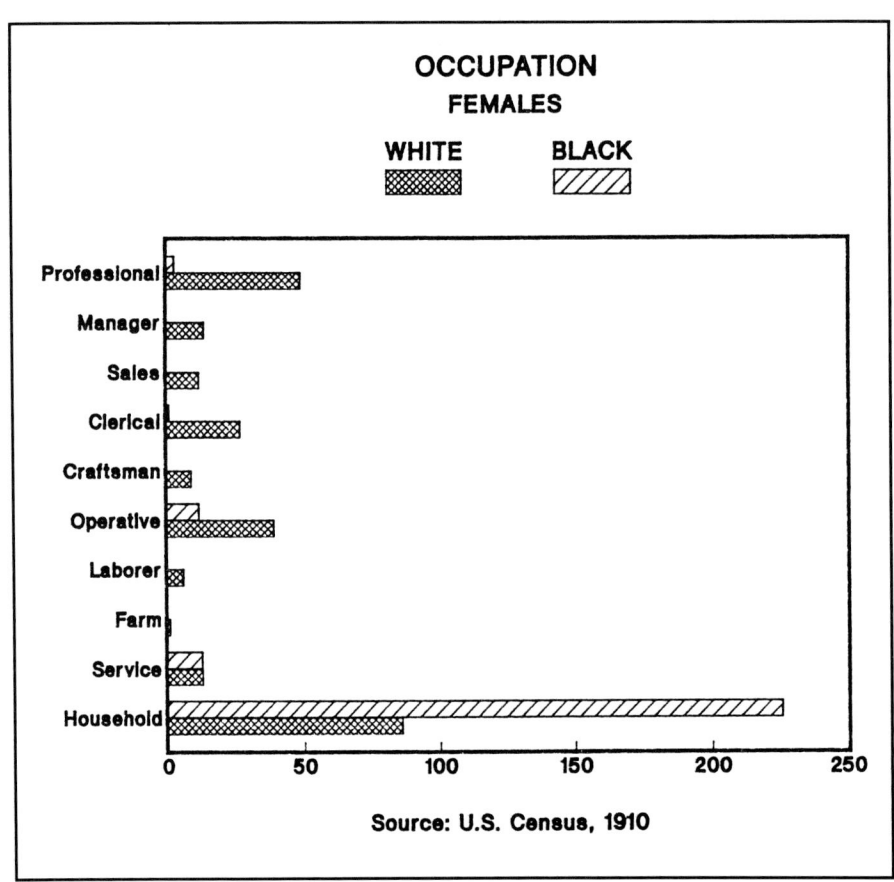

The 1910 Census: Work

While farming was on the wane as an occupational category in Catonsville by 1910, agriculture was still a part of village life. Reich's farm along Ingleside is shown circa 1895. Dorothy Maisel Reis

The 1910 Census: Place of Origin

Pfeiffer and Heinmuller children on the plank walk along Frederick Road, approximately 1909, their names evoking their German lineage. Left to right: Margaret Heinmuller, George Heinmuller, Madeline Pfeiffer with Charles Heinmuller in her arms, and Hilda Heinmuller.
Catonsville Room

The 1910 Census: Place of Origin

The family of Frederick Lentz, on the steps of their home at 734 Edmondson Avenue, about 1900. Mr. and Mrs. Lentz had immigrated from Germany in the 1880s.
Catonsville Room

The 1910 Census: Place of Origin

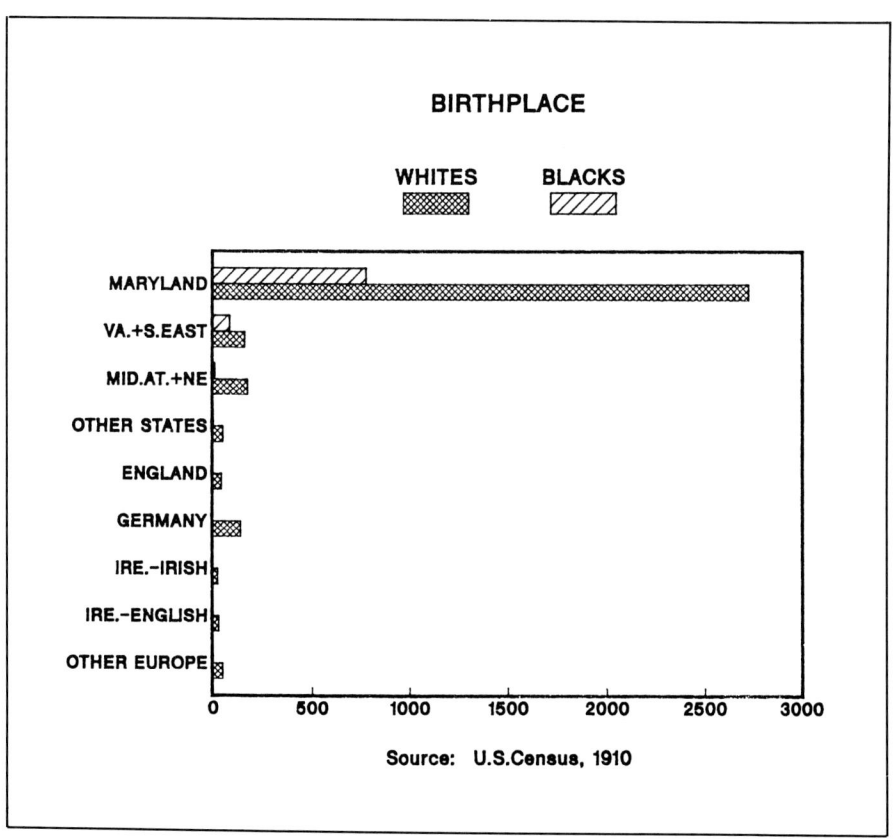

Information on place of origin in the 1910 manuscript census helps to trace ethnicity. The first column listed the person's place of birth (note here the double listings, such as "Ger-Germany" or "Ireland-Ire," which combined language identification with place, since linguistic or ethnic boundaries did not always coincide with national jurisdictions). The second and third columns gave the places of birth for the individual's father and mother, respectively. The fourth column noted the year when a foreign-born individual had immigrated to the United States (here two German-born individuals immigrated, one in 1885 and the other in 1872).

Whites and blacks were overwhelmingly of Maryland birth by 1910. Among whites, only about one in ten had been born abroad, with Germany the leading country of origin, as it had been in 1880. However, many Catonsville whites were the sons and daughters of immigrants; approximately one in three had fathers who had been born abroad, half of those in Germany.
Catonsville History Project, UMBC

The 1910 Census: Place of Origin

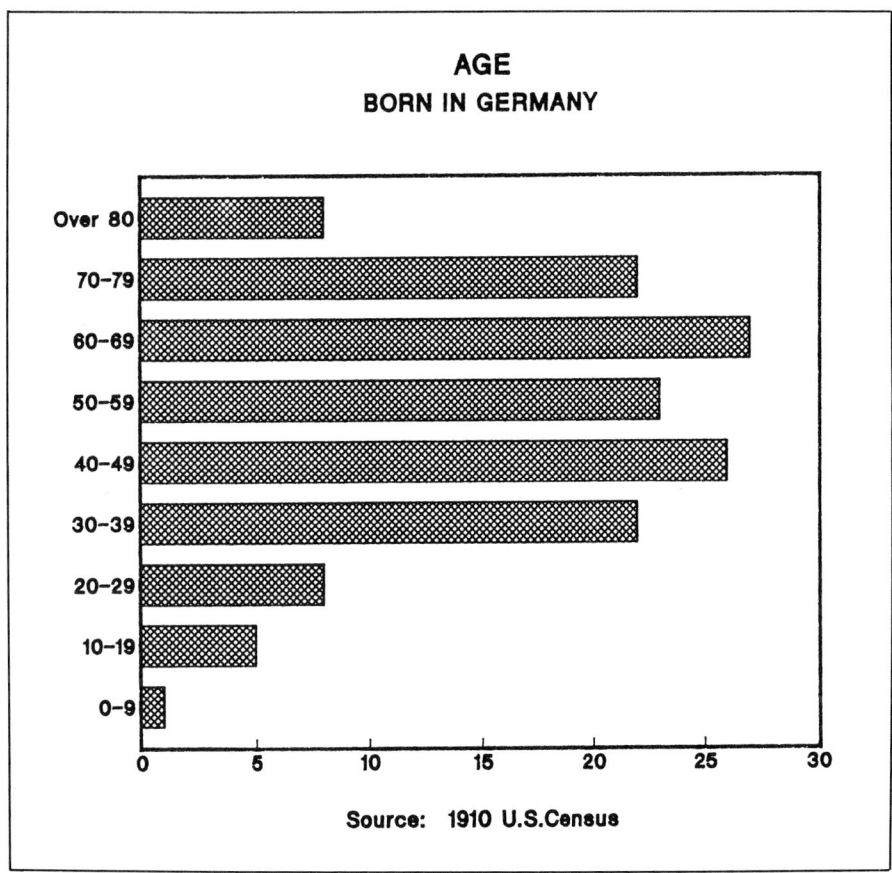

As one indication of the declining role of ethnicity, by 1910 most residents who had been born in Germany and immigrated to the United States were over thirty.
Catonsville History Project, UMBC

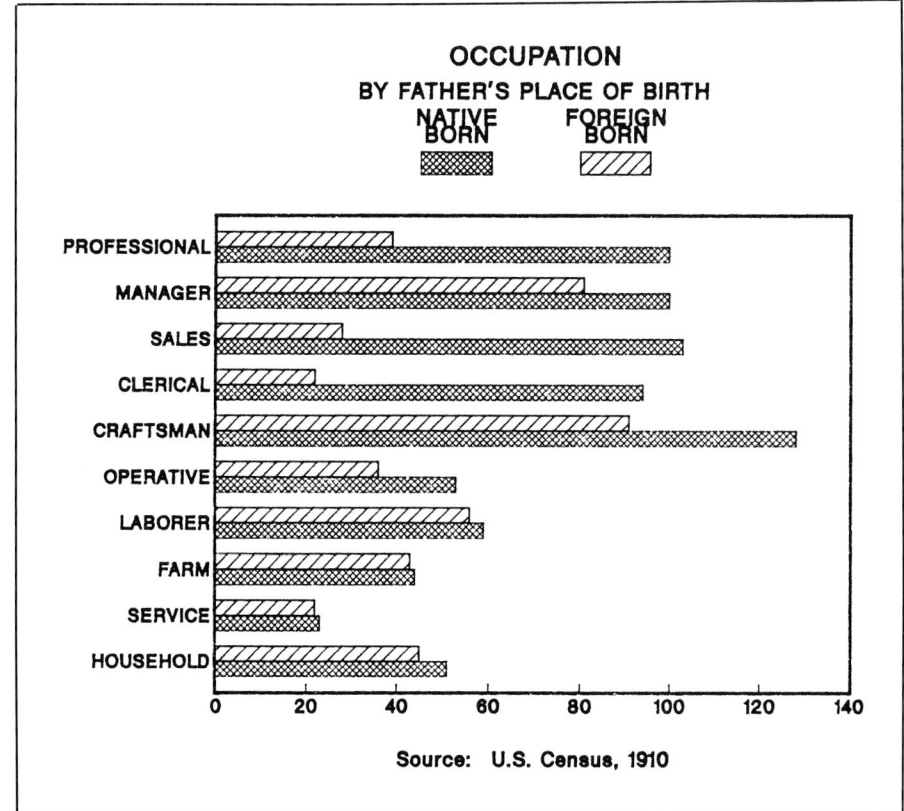

Ethnic background had slight impact on type of occupation. In the white-collar occupational categories, those whose fathers had been born abroad were more likely to be managers (entrepreneurs or supervisors) than professionals, salesmen, or clerical workers.

In general, those with foreign born fathers were more likely to be concentrated in blue-collar trades than those whose fathers were native born. In such occupational categories, they were strongly represented among craftsmen (skilled trades), with roughly equal numbers in other categories.
Catonsville History Project, UMBC

89

The 1910 Census: Race, School, and Homeownership

Domestics and children on the Ball family estate, Old Frederick Road, near Edmondson Avenue, no date.
Dorothy Maisel Reis

The 1910 Census: Race, School, and Homeownership

A class at the Catonsville School, Melrose Avenue and Winters Lane, poses formally about 1900.
Catonsville Room

John Harmon's report card from St. Mark Parish School, June, 1913 includes penmanship.
Ann Steffens

The 1910 Census: Race, School, and Homeownership

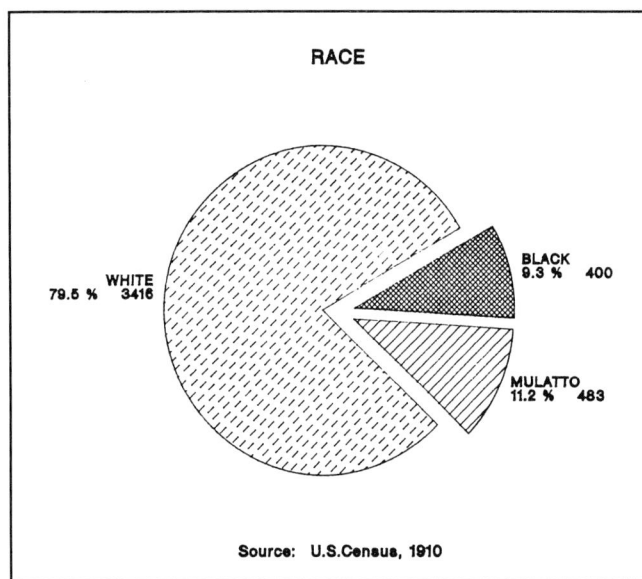

One-fifth of Catonsville's 1910 population was black. The census that year distinguished between black and mulatto (mixed racial parentage); the reliability of this distinction is unclear.
Catonsville History Project, UMBC

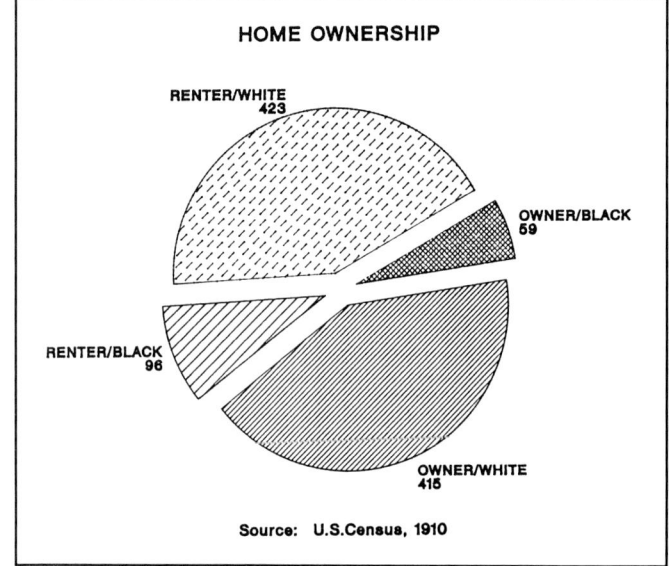

Approximately half of Catonsville's homes were owned by their residents. For whites, the percentage was slightly more than half, while for blacks one-third were homeowners.
Catonsville History Project, UMBC

On the eve of compulsory school attendance laws, most Catonsville youth between the ages of six and seventeen attended school, with little difference between boys and girls in this respect.
Catonsville History Project, UMBC

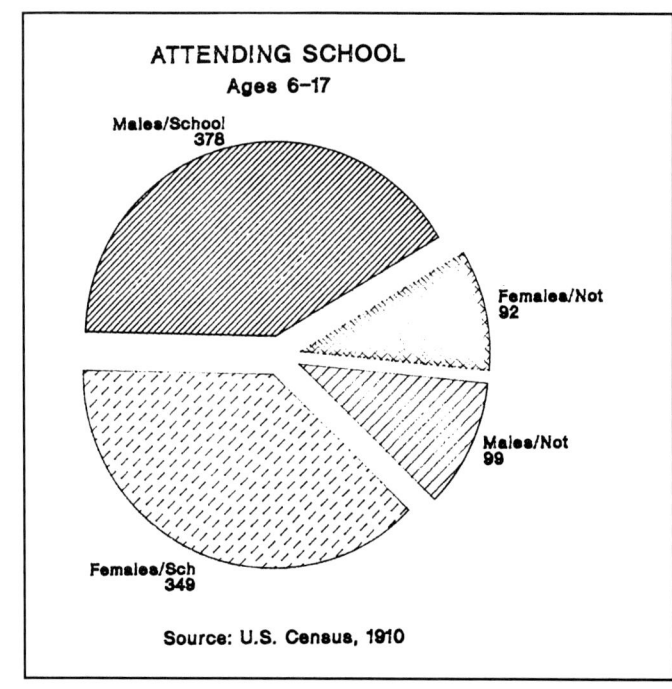

The 1910 Census: Race, School, and Homeownership

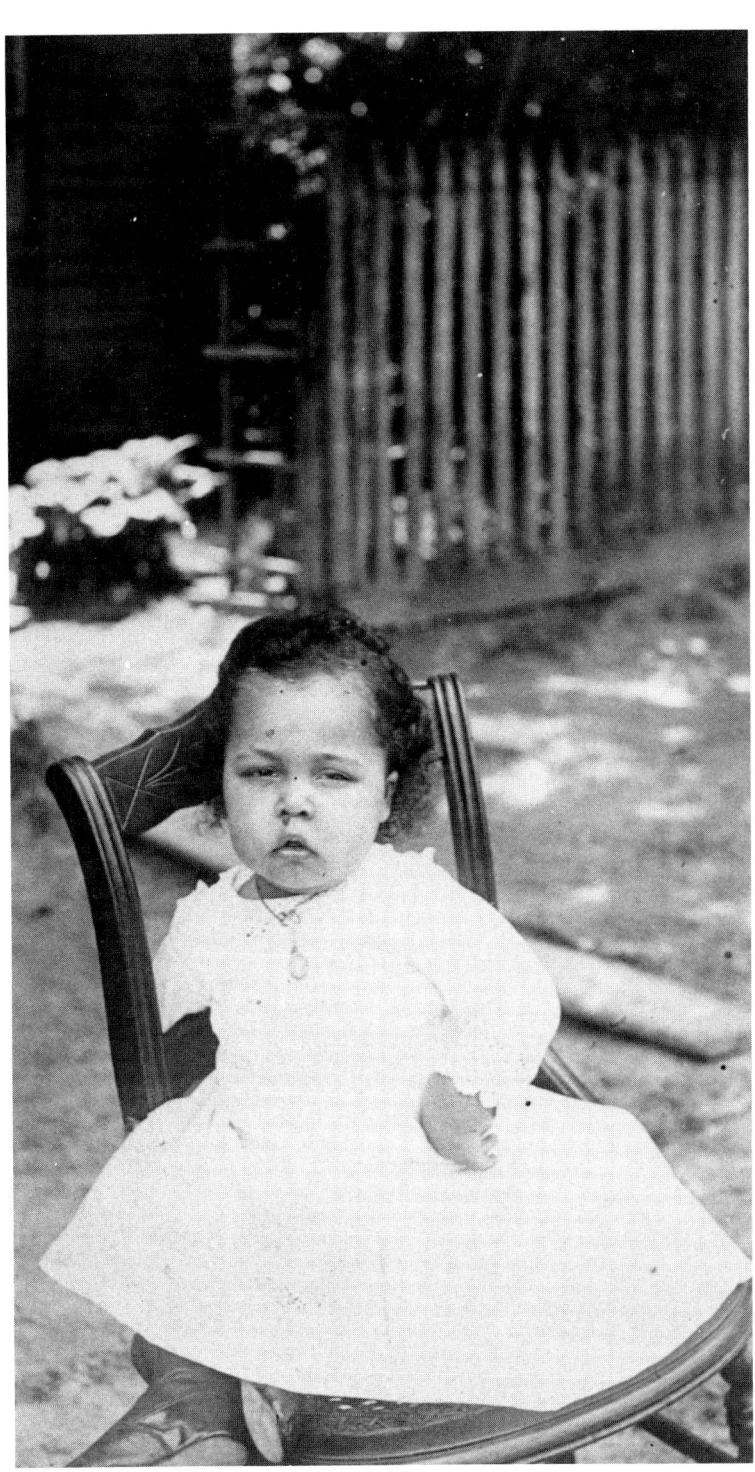

Willie Boston is booted and dressed as many little boys were circa 1900.
Mae Esther Coe

The Frederick Road Commercial Center, 1910 to 1916

Frederick Road, looking west from Ingleside Avenue, postcard, circa 1916. The photo shows passengers entering the No. 8 streetcar heading towards Baltimore. The line was electrified and double tracked out to Catonsville in 1895. Catonsville Room

The Frederick Road Commercial Center, 1910 to 1916

Frederick Road, looking west from Bloomsbury Avenue, circa 1910. Catonsville Room

The Frederick Road Commercial Center, 1910 to 1916

Frederick Road, looking east from Ingleside Avenue, circa 1915. On the left is the First National Bank of Catonsville.
Catonsville Room

A new streetcar for the No. 8 line (Frederick and York roads) stands ready to be put into service, circa 1910.
Baltimore Streetcar Museum Collection

The Frederick Road Commercial Center, 1910 to 1916

Frederick Road, looking east from Newburg Avenue, circa 1915. On the south side of the street are Salem Lutheran Church (far right) and the Masonic Hall, with the U.S. Post Office in the front.
Catonsville Room

Business Life on Frederick Road

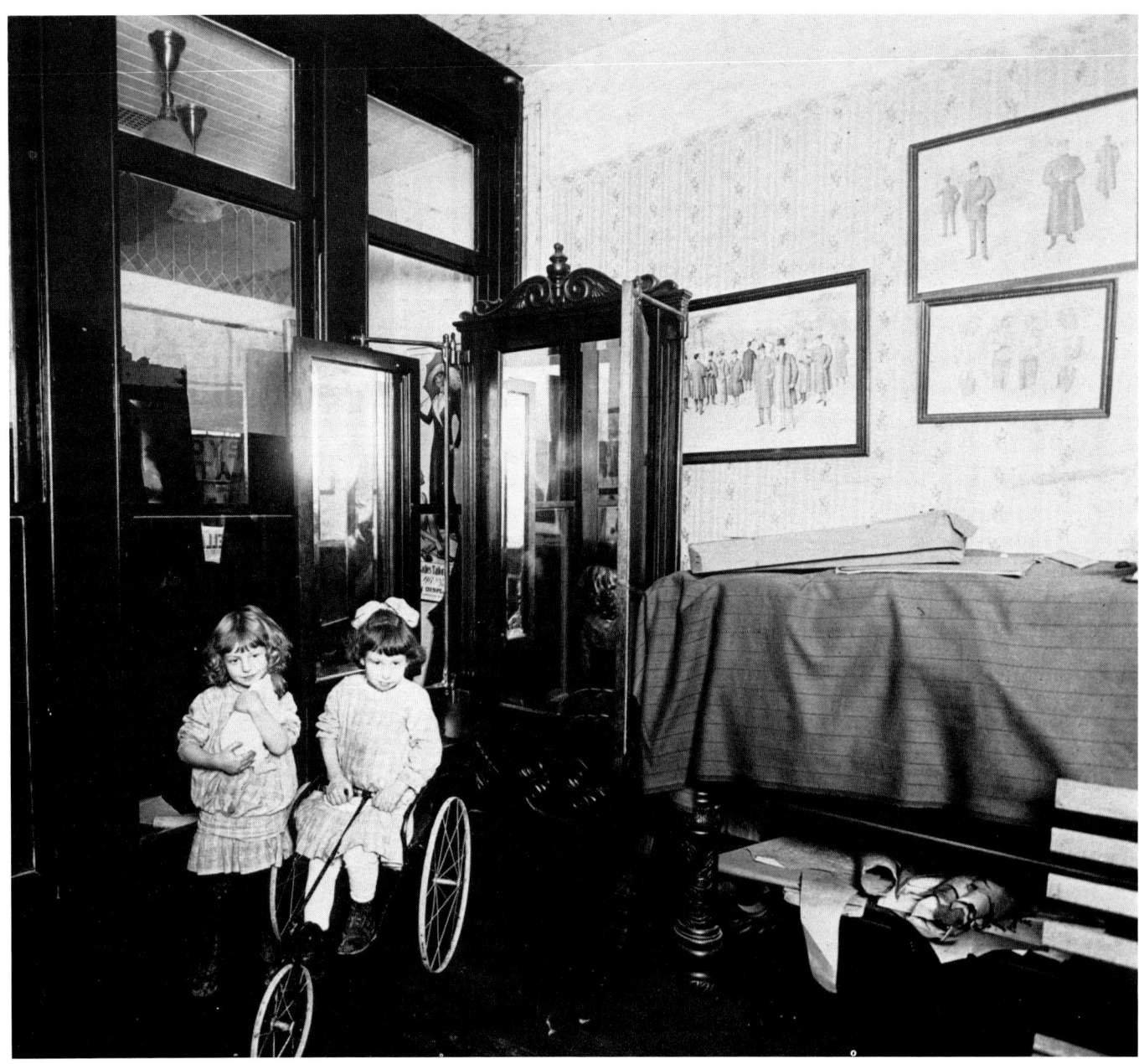

The tailoring establishment of Samuel R. Goldstein at 742 Frederick Road is pictured here in 1913 with Mr. Goldstein's two daughters, Bessie and Edna.

The manuscript census of 1910 showed the Samuel R. Goldstein family, residing at 806 Frederick Road, one block west of the shop known to area residents as "Sam the Tailor." It listed Mr. Goldstein as of "German Yiddish" birth and as having immigrated to the United States in 1886 at two years of age. It recorded that Mrs. Goldstein was born in New York. The ages of their daughters, Bessie and Edna, were entered, respectively, as one and "5/12" (i.e., 5 months).
Catonsville Room

Advertisement in The Argus, May 3, 1919. Samuel Goldstein sold his business later that same year, but the name "Sam the Tailor" was retained by the new proprietor.

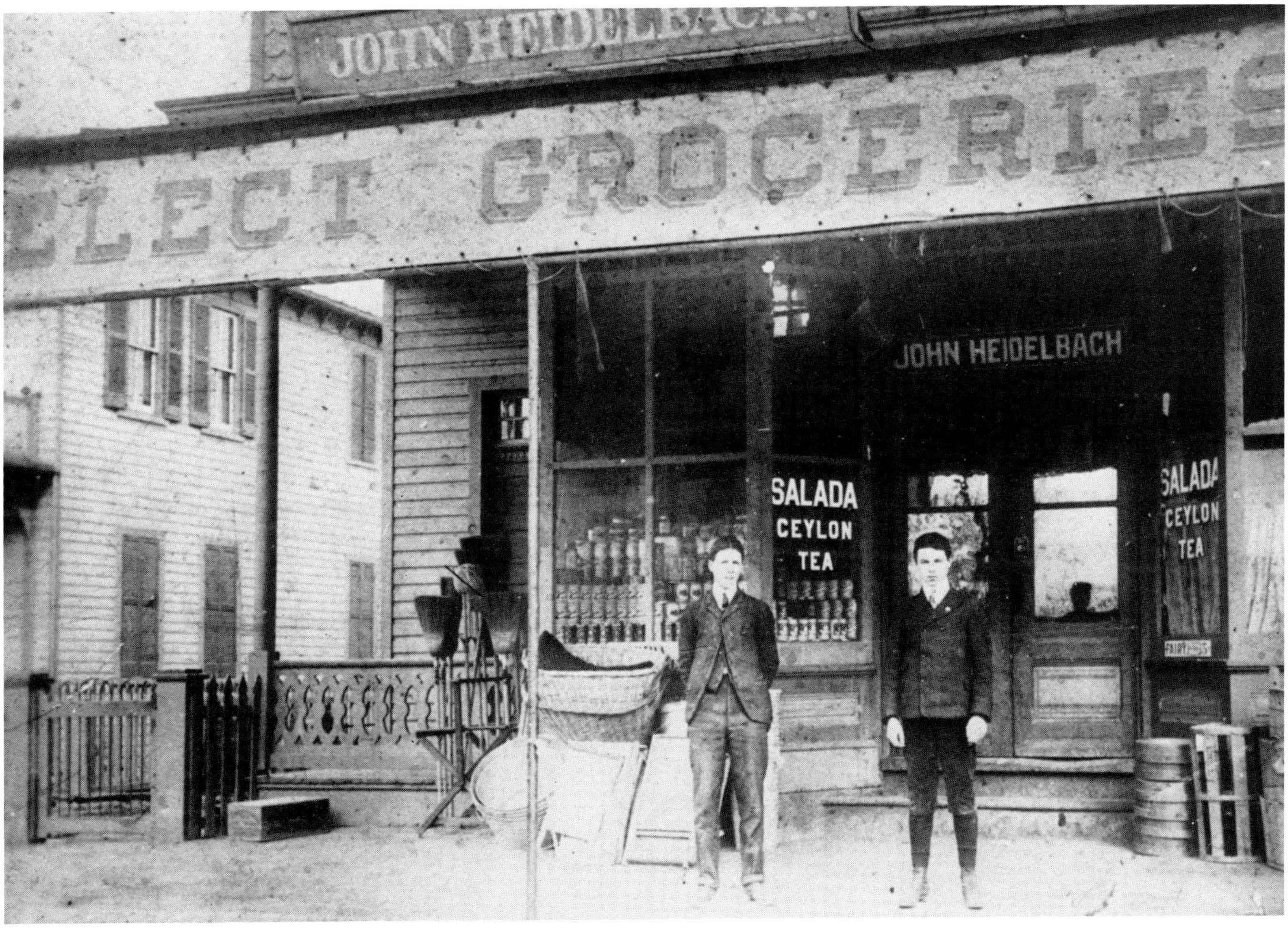
JOHN HEIDELBACH
LECT GROCERIES
JOHN HEIDELBACH
SALADA
CEYLON
TEA
SALADA
CEYLON
TEA

The Heidelbach grocery store in 1909 with William J. Heidelbach on the right. The 722 Frederick Road address was the second location for the store. The first store was at 918 Frederick Road from 1883 to 1889.
Catonsville Room

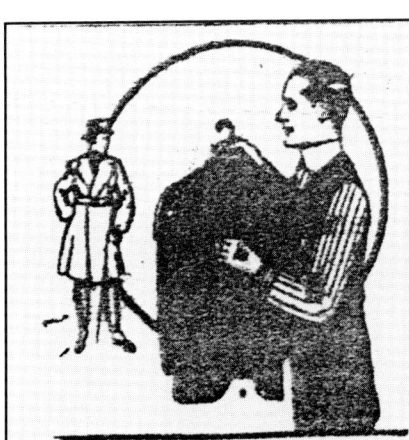

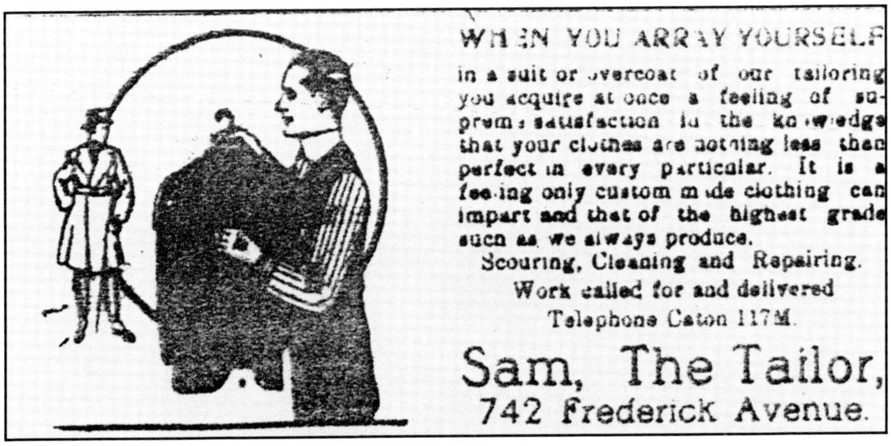
WHEN YOU ARRAY YOURSELF
in a suit or overcoat of our tailoring you acquire at once a feeling of supreme satisfaction in the knowledge that your clothes are nothing less than perfect in every particular. It is a feeling only custom made clothing can impart and that of the highest grade such as we always produce.
Scouring, Cleaning and Repairing.
Work called for and delivered
Telephone Caton 117M.
Sam, The Tailor,
742 Frederick Avenue.

Business Life on Frederick Road

John Peregoy and his son Frederick behind the counter of his grocery store at 833 Frederick Road in approximately 1910, the same year he served as census enumerator. The store previously had been John Grim's Flour, Feed, and Country Produce Store. Peregoy was married to Grim's daughter, Elizabeth. *Catonsville Room*

JOHN PEREGOY
Successor to JOHN GRIM,
Flour, Feed, Hay, Straw
and Country Produce.
833 Frederick Avenue, - Catonsville, Md.
Orders Promptly Delivered.

May 6 99 1y

Advertisement in the The Argus, *June 17, 1899.*

Business Life on Frederick Road

By the early 1900s, J. G. Owens occupied the front of the Library Hall building, his field and garden seeds catering to the mixed agricultural and suburban make up of the community. Note the mud of Frederick Road and the streetcar tracks in the foreground.
Catonsville Room; Elizabeth Peddicord

Business Life on Frederick Road

In 1911 the Harmon family acquired the dry goods store at 906 Frederick Road, formerly known as Burns'. In 1914 Harmon's added flowers to its line. The photo shows floral baskets in the window on the left and dry goods items in the window on the right.
Ann Steffens

Business Life on Frederick Road

M. A. HARMON,
DEALER IN
DRY GOODS, NOTIONS,
HOSIERY and UNDERWEAR
LADIES' AND CHILDREN'S READY-MADE CLOTHING
MEN'S FURNISHINGS
No. 906 FREDERICK AVENUE, CATONSVILLE.

GOODS NOT IN STOCK WILL BE SECURED ON SHORT NOTICE.

C. & P. Phone 116W.   M. A. HARMON, Prop.

Advertisement in The Argus, *August 10, 1912. Note that M. A. Harmon is Mrs. Mary Agnes Harmon.*

Phone Caton 116W

Flowers for Easter

You can make the best selection here, secure prompt and courteous attention and pay the lowest price.
We solicit your earliest patronage.

JOHN B. HARMON, Florist

906 Frederick Ave., Catonsville

Advertisement in The Argus, *April 22, 1916. Note that the business was then listed in the husband's name, John B. Harmon.*

Streetcar Housing Developments, 1900 to 1918

This sign advertises Oak Forest Park at the intersection of Frederick Road and Montrose Avenue, circa 1918. At the end of World War I, developments like this one were poised for new growth. The sign lists the developer for this new portion of Oak Forest Park as J. W. Holloway. *Catonsville Room*

Streetcar Housing Developments, 1900 to 1918

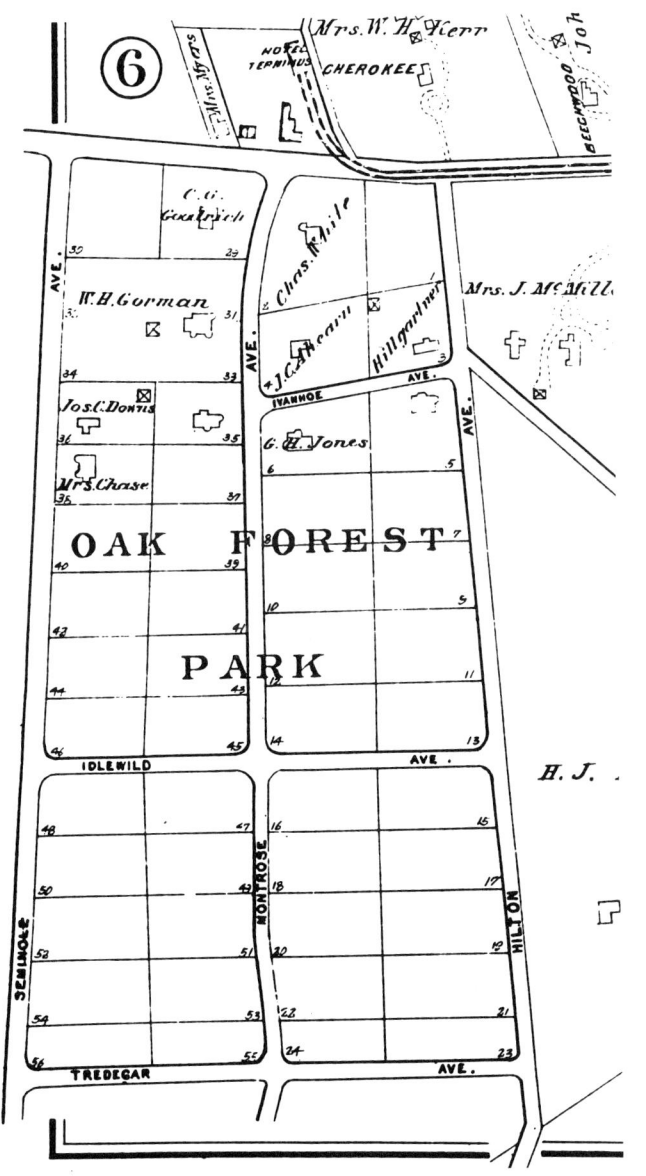

This advertisement for Forest Spring Park, developed by H. Clay Suter on land formerly part of the Lurman estate, appeared in The Argus, *July 27, 1912.*

This detail of Oak Forest Park is from the 1898 Bromley Atlas. The original development, with its large and spacious lots, was begun by the Catonsville Improvement Company. John Hubner was the company's president in the early years.

Until it was annexed by Baltimore City in 1918, Ten Hills was considered a Catonsville area "country suburb." Ten Hills was developed from the former Chappell estate by Caughy, Hearn, and Carter. It fronted on Edmondson Avenue, along which the No. 9 and No. 14 streetcars traveled from downtown Baltimore to Catonsville Junction and the No. 9 on to Ellicott City.
The Argus, *August 19, 1912.*

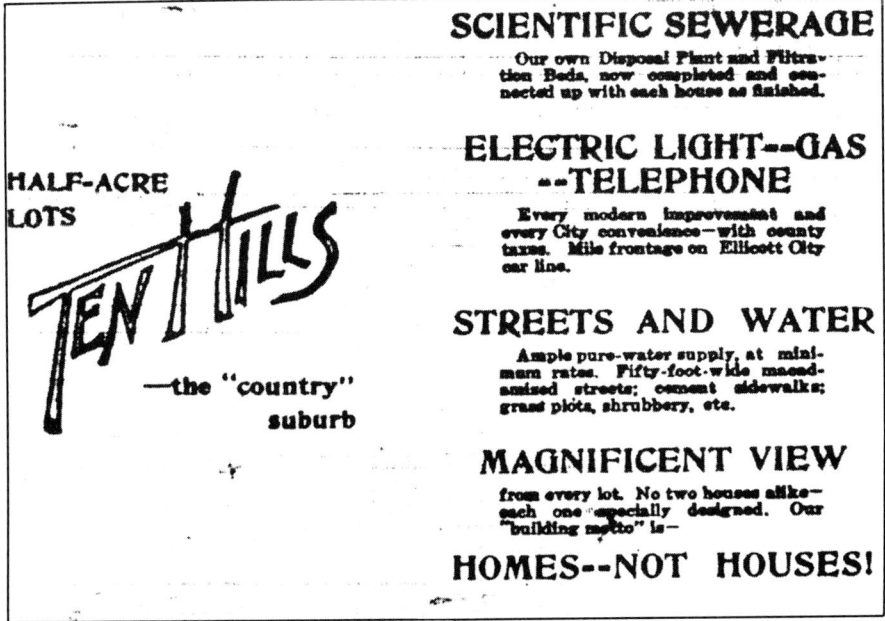

Developments, 1900 to 1918 Streetcar Housing

Smaller, independent builders such as John Gerwig constructed many individual dwellings in and around Catonsville during these years. Gerwig built this home, pictured in approximately 1910, at 119 Smithwood Avenue for the Bockmiller family. Left to right are Elizabeth Bockmiller, holding Leonard; Richard B. (on toy); and Richard R.

The 1910 manuscript census identified the residents of 119 Smithwood Avenue as Richard R. Bockmiller (age 37) and his wife Barbara E. (Elizabeth) (43), with their sons Richard B. (1) and L. (Leonard) (2/12, i.e., 2 months).
Catonsville Room

Frederick Maisel, Jr., was another significant, independent builder active in house construction during this era. The sign in his yard at 517 Ingleside Avenue advertised his business.
Dorothy Maisel Reis

The new Catonsville High School, circa 1910, on Frederick Road, just east of Bloomsbury Avenue. It replaced the former structure at Melrose Avenue and Winters Lane, and housed all of the elementary and secondary school grades for the community's white youth. Today the structure serves as Catonsville Elementary School.
Catonsville Room

Catonsville's black children continued to attend the Catonsville Colored School at the northeast corner of Edmondson and Winters Lane. An article from *The Argus*, dated June 29, 1907, reported local opposition to turning the old Catonsville School at Melrose Avenue and Winters Lane over for use as the Colored School when a new structure would be erected for the community's white children:

STATUS OF SCHOOL QUESTION.
Much Opposition to Present Building Being Turned Over to Colored Children

Governor Warfield's criticism of the public school building at Catonsville at the high school commencement here last week, has had the effect to urge the committee of citizens having the erection of a new high school building in charge to renewed efforts.

Governor Warfield took occasion to score Catonsvillians for their lack of interest in cooperating with the school committee in securing a suitable site for the school and said that he hoped that by the next commencement season he would see the building completed or at least under way.

The school committee has experienced much difficulty in securing a site for the new school, as stated in *The Argus* several weeks ago. Options on two pieces of property were secured and the matter had progressed as far as the purchase of the property on Frederick avenue, occupied by Mr. C. Willing Browne, for the new school, which the county board had pledged to erect if the residents purchased the grounds, but property owners in the neighborhood objected so strenuously to the school being near them that the site was abandoned. The title of the other property on which an option was secured, prohibited its sale to other than private interests.

The opposition to the new school is largely on account of the use to which the old school building will be put to. The colored school children of the village have outgrown their present quarters and it is the intention of the school board to turn over to the colored children the white school. This would bring the colored children almost into the heart of the village and white residents and property owners in the neighborhood say that it would mean a sure decrease in property values, besides bringing to their door an objectionable element. They claim that the present white school could be enlarged to suit the needs of the community for one-third the cost of a new building and that if more grounds were needed there is property available on both the north and east sides of the school grounds.

About seven years ago over $10,000 was expended on the present school in enlarging and modernizing it, and the building is up-to-date in every particular.

Schooling in the New Century

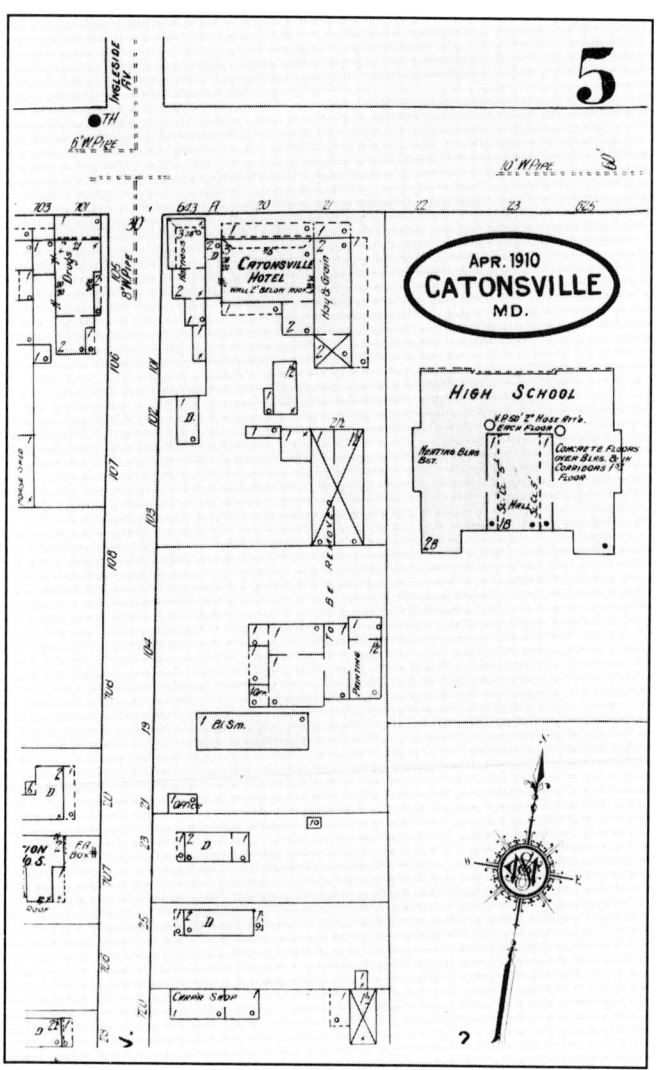

This detail from the Sanborn Fire Insurance Map of Catonsville, April, 1910, shows the new brick structure of the high school and notes the relevant fire security information. Next door, near the corner of Frederick and Bloomsbury, was the Catonsville Hotel.
Map Division, Library of Congress

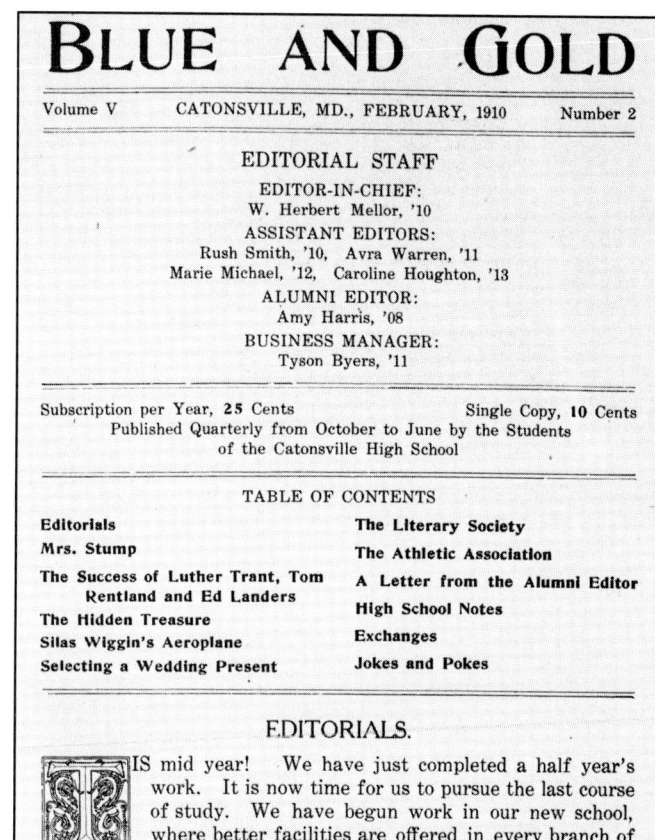

On the cover of the school's literary journal, Blue and Gold, February 1910, the editorial admonished, "Let this first year of work in our new building be a success."
Catonsville Room

Schooling in the New Century

Cover of the program for the dedication of the new Catonsville High School building, April 29, 1910.
Catonsville Room

Schooling in the New Century

Faculty

Mr. Rene Edward de Russy   Miss Hannah Scott   Miss Helen Coulter   Miss Mary Ebaugh

Miss Ada Colburn   Miss Edith Tracey   Miss Reba Neepier   Mr. Clarence Edward Earle

The faculty of Catonsville High School is depicted in the school's yearbook, The June Bug, *1914.*
Catonsville Room

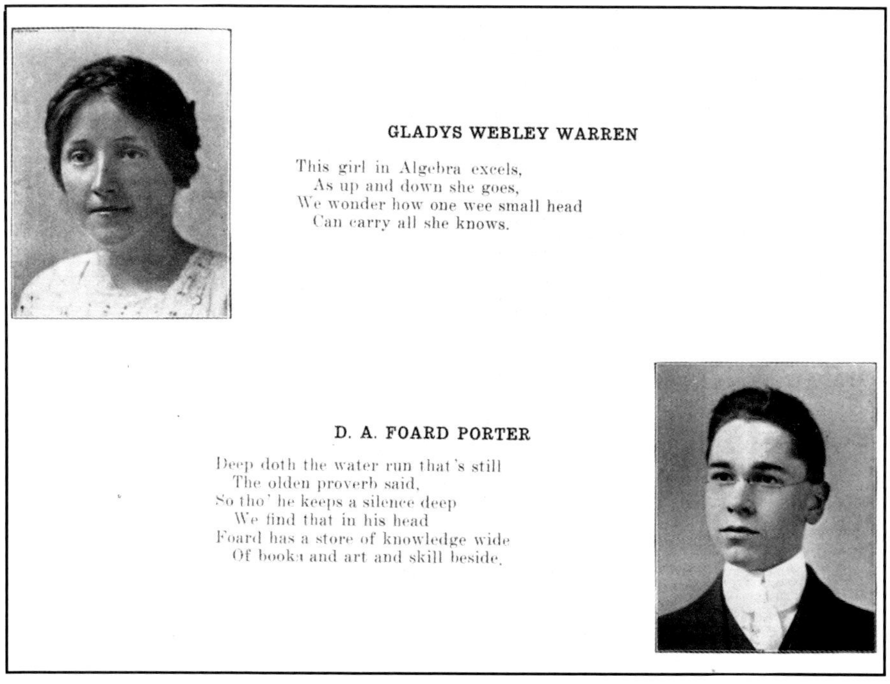

The June Bug, *1914, included photos of graduating seniors, along with humorous poems characterizing each. Pictured here are those for Gladys Webley Warren and D. A. Foard Porter.*
Catonsville Room

GLADYS WEBLEY WARREN

This girl in Algebra excels,
  As up and down she goes,
We wonder how one wee small head
  Can carry all she knows.

D. A. FOARD PORTER

Deep doth the water run that's still
  The olden proverb said,
So tho' he keeps a silence deep
  We find that in his head
Foard has a store of knowledge wide
  Of books and art and skill beside.

Schooling in the New Century

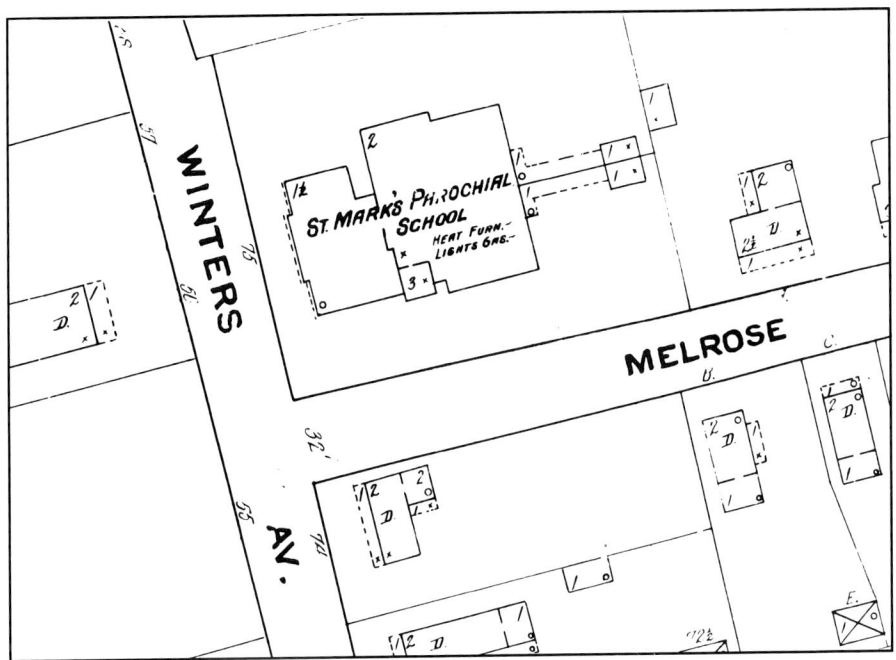

The Sanborn Fire Insurance Company Map of Catonsville for 1910 shows that the old Catonsville School had become St. Mark Parish School, conveniently located a block from the parish church. The sale of the building to St. Mark's resolved the controversy over the use of the old school. However, the question of adequate facilities for black children would not be satisfactorily addressed until the 1920s when the county erected a new brick facility at Wesley and Main Avenues, though education was still on a segregated basis.
Map Division, Library of Congress

Edgar Alexander Coe is pictured in a late 1910s yearbook of the Baltimore City Colored High School (named in the early 1920s for Frederick Douglass). Since Baltimore County had no high schools for black youth, Coe, who lived on Winters Lane in Catonsville, attended this segregated city secondary school to complete his education.
Mae Esther Coe

Social Life in the 1900s and 1910s

Catonsville Baseball Club, early decades
of the twentieth century.
Dorothy Maisel Reis

Social Life in the 1900s and 1910s

Baseball at Suter Field, undated.
Dorothy Maisel Reis

Social Life in the 1900s and 1910s

Five gentlemen pose in front of the Odd Fellows Hall on Ingleside Avenue, about 1918 to 1920. Identified here in the back row, left to right, are Jake Reich, Jesse Chamberlain, and Shorty Ruff; in the front row are Christian Diehlmann and Daniel Diehlmann.
Catonsville Room

Social Life in the 1900s and 1910s

The Pot and Kettle Club, its members pictured here on February 12, 1915, at a masquerade party, was a prominent, local social organization.
Catonsville Room

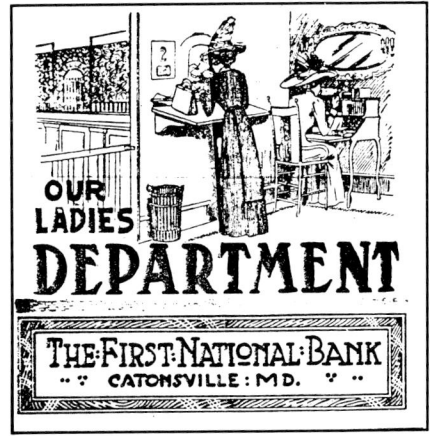

Advertisement in The Argus, *July 18, 1917. The bank boasted a "Ladies Department" as a special feature when it opened its new building in 1902.*

Advertisement in The Argus, *April 27, 1918.*

Social Life in the 1900s and 1910s

A 1908 Pierce-Arrow automobile with a young man named Seicke at the wheel, is pictured in front of the gatehouse to the Ingleside estate, built by Bernard Baker in 1892 and sold to developer Anthony Carozza in 1919. The gatehouse was on the northwest corner of old Frederick Road and Ingleside Avenue (now the intersection of Route 40 and Ingleside); in the late 1950s the site of the estate house was developed as the Westview Shopping Center.
Catonsville Room

A Winters Lane Family: The Coes

On May 25, 1911, Livous and Annie Coe contracted to build a two-story home at 67 Winters Lane. The new home is pictured here, shortly after completion.
Mae Esther Coe

Livous A. Coe and Annie Boston Coe pose in the backyard of their home at 67 Winters Lane in 1915. Livous worked as a gardener near Carroll Station, while Annie worked as a laundress for local estate families. The Coe and Boston families had deep roots in Catonsville's black community.
Mae Esther Coe

A Winters Lane Family: The Coes

Livous A. Coe and Annie E. Boston were married on December 16, 1896, at Grace African Methodist Episcopal Church on Winters Lane, where they were life-long members. Shown is their marriage certificate.
Mae Esther Coe

The contract with the local building firm of Schatz Brothers called for the payment of $1,575 for the Coes' new home.
Mae Esther Coe

A Winters Lane Family: The Coes

Annie Boston (later Coe) seated on the porch with her mother, Elizabeth Boston (seated, center foreground), and sisters Mary Rebecca (left) and Florence (right). They are pictured at the Boston's home on the corner of Wade Avenue (then Asylum Lane) and Fairview Avenue, where Thomas and Elizabeth owned several houses inhabited by other black families.
Mae Esther Coe

In 1880 the manuscript census listed Livous (spelled "Lives" by the enumerator) as a boy of thirteen. The family included his sister, Secilia (age fifteen); his mother, Rachel A. (forty-eight) who kept house; and his father, Alexander (fifty-nine) who worked as a gardener, just as Livous later would do.

The Boston family Bible recorded the birth of Anna Elizabeth (the two names written together) to Thomas and Elizabeth Boston on August 20, 1872. Also listed are George Washington, Mary Rebecca ("Maryrebecker"), and Florence Corteller. Note, too, the record of a family death in 1868 on the upper left hand page.
Mae Esther Coe

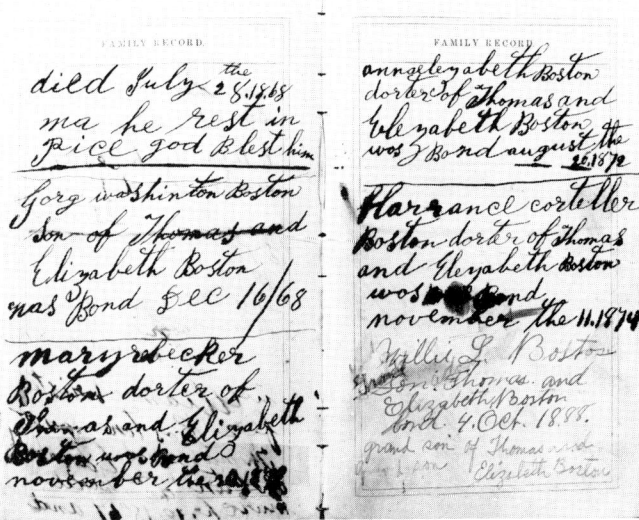

A Winters Lane Family: The Coes

Mae Esther Coe, daughter of Livous and Annie, pictured in approximately 1920 in a coat made for her by her mother. Mae completed the eighth grade at the Catonsville Colored School, then graduated from Frederick Douglass High School in Baltimore City. In the late 1920s she received her degree from Cheyney State College in Pennsylvania. Returning to Baltimore County, she taught in one room schools for black children, first in Monkton and then in Halethorpe, until World War II.
Mae Esther Coe

Mae's brother, Edgar Alexander Coe, pictured here with his classmates when he completed the eighth grade at the Catonsville Colored School. Edgar, as Mae would do later, continued his secondary school education in Baltimore City.
Mae Esther Coe

A Winters Lane Family: The Coes

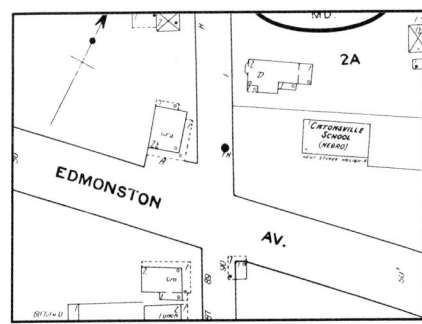

The family of Livous and Annie Coe on the front porch of their new Winters Lane home about 1913. Pictured left to right are Livous A. (Sr.), Mae Esther (seated on her mother's lap), Annie, Livous Boston (foreground), and Edgar Alexander. Census enumerator John Peregoy listed the family members' ages in 1910 as Livous (Sr.) (forty); Annie (thirty-five); Edgar (Alexander) (twelve); Livous (Boston) (nine); and (Mae) Esther (four).
Mae Esther Coe

Only a short distance from the Coe family home, the corner of Edmondson Avenue and Winters Lane served as the center of the black community when Mae was growing up. This 1910 Sanborn Fire Insurance Company map shows the frame "Catonsville School, Negro" on the northeast corner, noting that it had "heat stove, no lights." Several grades had to be housed across the street in the Mt. Olivet Methodist Church on Edmondson Avenue (not pictured) and in Williams' Store, on the southwest corner of Winters Lane and Edmondson.

The intersection's two grocery stores, Williams' and Shockett's (on the northwest corner), provided both commercial services and meeting places for members of the black community.
McKeldin Library, University of Maryland College Park

Mae Coe and her brother, Edgar Alexander, are pictured here with cousins Horace and Horace, Jr., in front of the Coe family home at 67 Winters Lane in approximately 1930.

During World War II, Mae left teaching to take a job with the federal government in Washington, D.C., first with the Census Bureau and later with the State Department. She commuted by train to work from her Winters Lane home for two decades until her retirement in the early 1960s.
Mae Esther Coe

121

*For many years the end of the No. 8 streetcar line was the Terminal Hotel on Frederick Road, shown here in 1918 behind the car station. In 1918 the streetcar tracks were extended along a private right of way to Catonsville Junction on Edmondson Avenue, where the Nos. 9 and 14 ran. Passengers could thus transfer between these three lines.
Catonsville Room*

Chapter V

The Auto Era, 1920 to 1940

The decades of boom and bust are clearly reflected in the history of Catonsville, but the extremes of this era are muted because the community became dominated by middle income residents. As the population grew dramatically, the percentage of the very rich and the relatively poor families both declined during the 1920s, making the community more economically homogeneous.

By the 1920s very few of the wealthy families that were so prominent in the Victorian era made Catonsville their home—even in the summer. The sale of the Summit estate in 1921 and its subsequent development by the Mohler brothers as a middle-income subdivision called Summit Park signaled the passing of an era. At the other end of the income scale, many of the town's working-class white families became more comfortable, and even the local black residents, in spite of continuing educational and job discrimination, made noticeable economic progress.

On the other hand, the general boom in real estate drove both land and construction costs upwards, and those who could not accumulate enough funds to buy a building lot or enough steady income to obtain a mortgage found it difficult to live in Catonsville. The Winters Lane black community, almost surrounded by established white neighborhoods, had very little room for expansion.

The prosperity of the decade and the suburban trend of Baltimore City families brought an unprecedented volume of new home construction—and new people—to Catonsville. The population

The Auto Era, 1920 to 1940

jumped from approximately five thousand in 1920 to over nine thousand in 1930 as almost nine hundred new dwellings were built in the old town and in new subdivisions farther away from the Frederick Road core area. The land between Eden Terrace (where the Baltimore Beltway now cuts through the community) and the 1918 Baltimore City Line became densely built up with modest cottage and bungalow style dwellings.

Community prosperity and rapid population growth made the 1920s an era of new school construction. In 1923 black students were transferred from the old dilapidated Catonsville Colored School to a modern brick structure several blocks away at Wesley and Main avenues. White school-age enrollment expansion led to construction of the new high school on Bloomsbury Avenue in 1925, only fifteen years after erection of the Frederick Road facility.

The streetcar lines on Frederick Road and Edmondson Avenue remained quite important; but from World War I onwards the automobile began to have a significant impact. Automobile dealerships appeared on Frederick Road and on several of the side streets. By the late 1920s the old Short Line depot had become an auto repair shop. The glamour of the Jazz Age was shared by Catonsville, at least vicariously, by watching the latest Hollywood movies at the Alpha Theater, which opened in 1928.

The stock market crash of 1929 hit home when the Catonsville branch of the Union Trust Bank failed in March, 1933. Almost no new houses were built in the community again until 1938. Since the town did not have a large blue-collar work force, there were no soup kitchens, but many families were hurt deeply by the Depression. Local newspapers, *The Argus* and the new *Catonsville Herald*, carried a number of announcements for fund raisers to help the unemployed needy of the town and the surrounding area. Some homeowners were forced to pay only the interest on their mortgages since they lacked the money to continue paying the principal.

There was, however, a positive side to the local picture in the 1930s. The Depression appeared to bring people closer together and to encourage a greater spirit of cooperation. There was a major "Buy in Catonsville" campaign to support the local merchants, but a number of them were forced out of business by the hard times. When the New Deal's National Recovery Administration (NRA) urged merchants to hire more employees and to close on Wednesday afternoons, there was almost universal cooperation along Frederick Road. On one particular Sunday in 1934, all the town churches urged their members to support the NRA effort to restore prosperity. The lack of income encouraged a more inexpensive social life. The newspapers were filled with articles about the activities of numerous local social clubs, and community-wide events took on special importance. For example, a crowd of some five hundred people gathered in 1933 for the first annual lighting of the community Christmas tree at the corner of Frederick Road and Melvin Avenue.

As the Depression began to lift in 1938 and 1939, building activity reappeared on lots that had stood vacant for a decade. The local economy returned to a point very near its former level of prosperity, only to be interrupted in 1941 by the extraordinary dislocations of World War II.

The decades of the 1920s and 1930s wrought significant changes in Catonsville. The "boom" years of the 1920s added an unprecedented number of new houses and new people to the community. While this development established even more firmly its predominantly middle-class character, the influx of residents tended to change its village atmosphere. The "bust" decade of the 1930s forced both the newcomers and older residents to live on tight budgets and to help one another cope with the hard times. The growth of social organizations and community events in both decades suggested a renewed quest for identity and sociability. By 1940 Catonsville had become a full-fledged suburban town, but a suburb where residents had rekindled a sense of community life that had been part of its earlier village existence.

Catonsville Fire Insurance Maps, July 1925

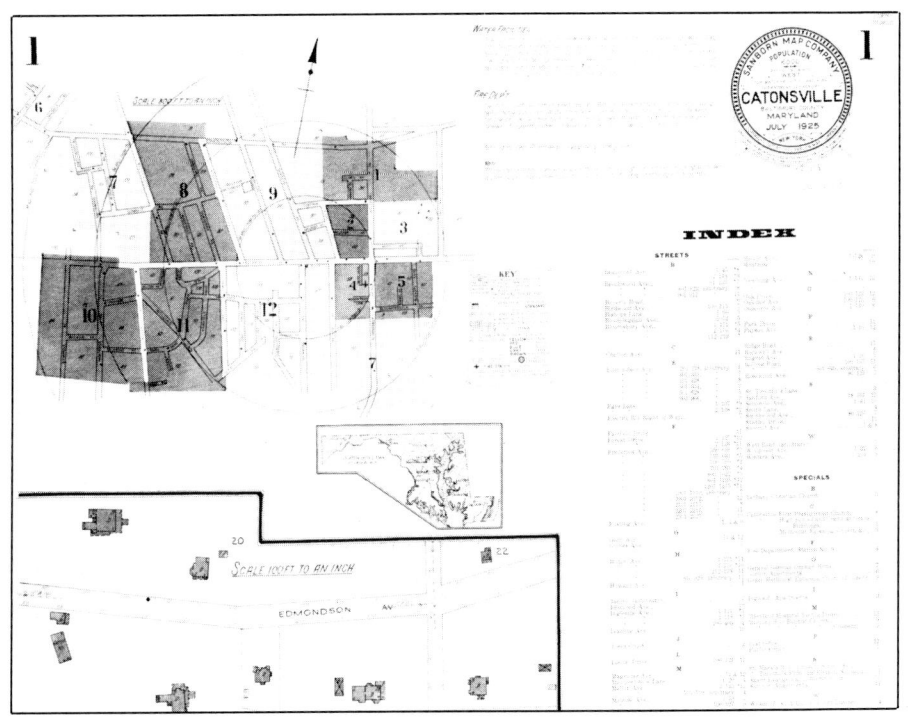

The Sanborn Fire Insurance Company map of 1925 shows the steady enlargement of Catonsville, using twelve sections rather than the six sections used in its 1910 atlas. Pictured here is the map key to the twelve sections.
Maryland Department, McKeldin Library, University of Maryland College Park

The John S. Wilson Company expanded to the west on the site of the old Library Hall. Immediately to the east of the firm's lumber yards, an auto service garage had opened, providing innovative off-street gas pumps, one of many indications in the 1925 maps of the importance of the auto.
Maryland Department, McKeldin Library, University of Maryland College Park

Catonsville Fire Insurance Maps, July 1925

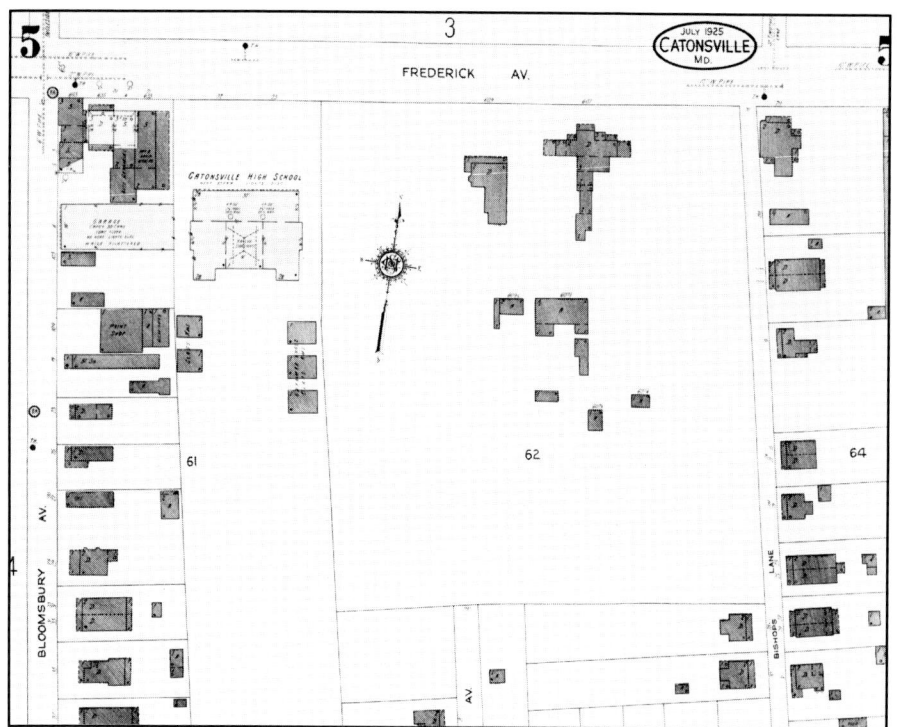

In only fifteen years the Catonsville High School had outgrown its building. Even with five temporary classrooms added in the rear of the structure, the school could not hold the rapidly increasing number of students. Next door, the Catonsville Hotel had ceased operation, and behind it was a garage with a capacity for thirty cars, another sign of the new auto age.
Maryland Department, McKeldin Library, University of Maryland College Park

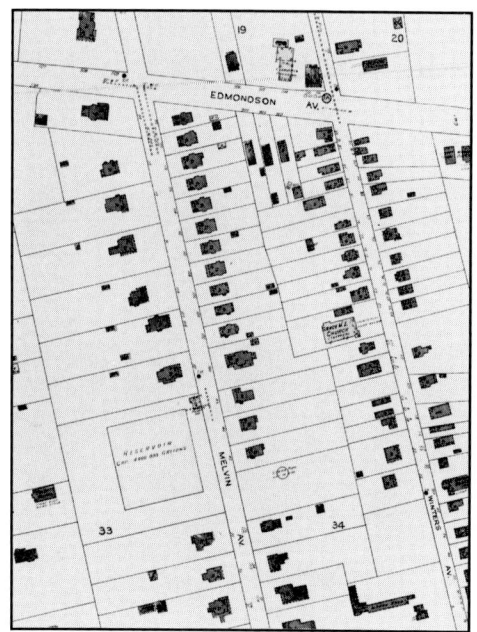

By the 1920s builders were constructing rows of detached houses quite similar in their basic plan, like these bungalows along Melvin Avenue south of Edmondson. Nineteen of twenty-eight houses on Melvin have garages, indicating a high proportion of automobile ownership by Catonsville's suburban residents. In contrast, only three of thirty-eight dwellings shown here along Winters Lane have garages.
Maryland Department, McKeldin Library, University of Maryland College Park

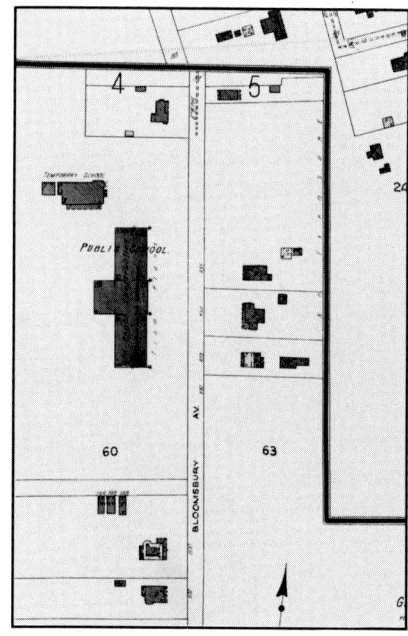

The new Catonsville High School, identified here as "Public School," is shown as nearly completed. The structure was built on Bloomsbury Avenue on the grounds of the old Catonsville Country Club. Initially the clubhouse, just north of the new school, was used for the school's dining hall on the ground floor, while the principal and his family lived upstairs.
Maryland Department, McKeldin Library, University of Maryland College Park

Catonsville Fire Insurance Maps, March 1930

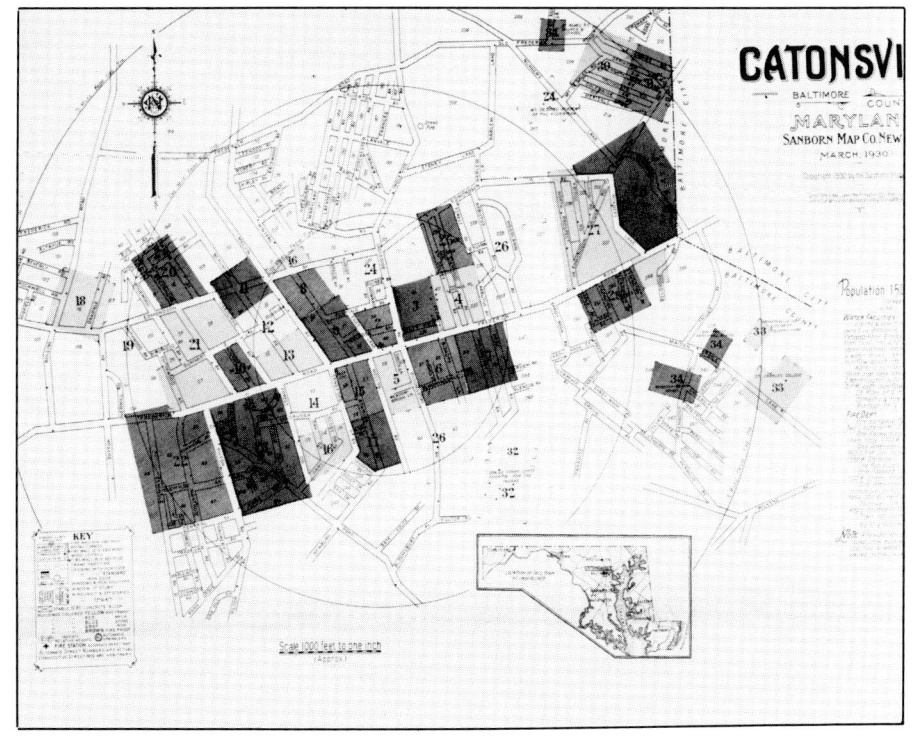

The Sanborn Fire Insurance map of March, 1930, shows a much larger community than portrayed in the 1925 map. It now required thirty-four sheets to cover Catonsville's residential and commercial developments, compared to only twelve in 1925. The mapmaker estimated the population to be fifteen thousand.
Maryland Department, McKeldin Library, University of Maryland College Park

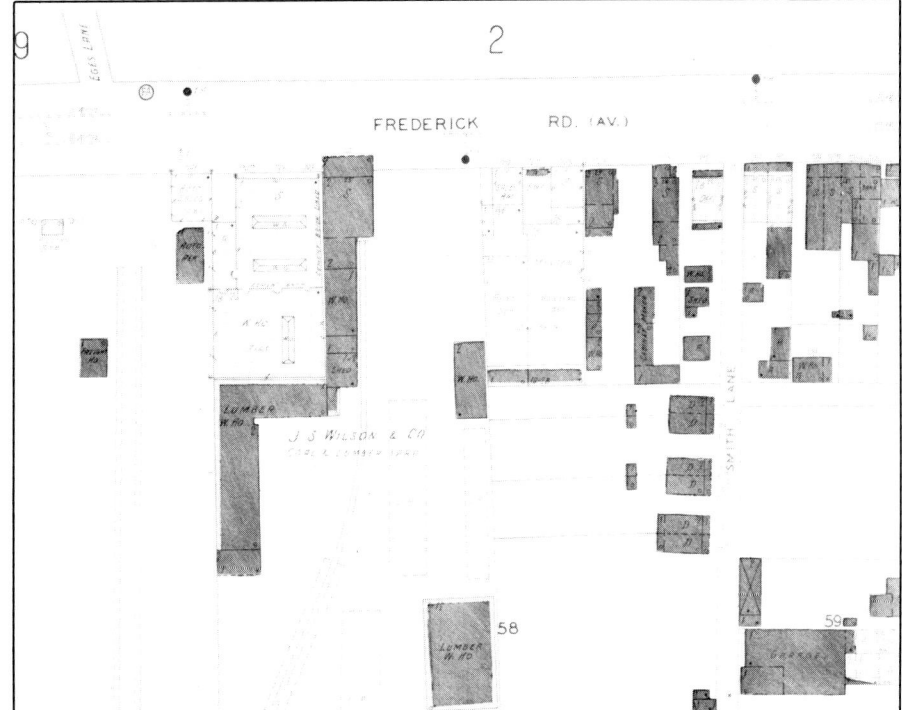

This detail from Map 5 shows the John S. Wilson Lumber Company and the shops on the south side of Frederick Road. The "movies" is the Alpha Theater, opened in 1928. Three auto sales or repair shops are shown, one of them occupying the old Short Line depot.
Maryland Department, McKeldin Library, University of Maryland College Park

Catonsville Fire Insurance Maps, March 1930

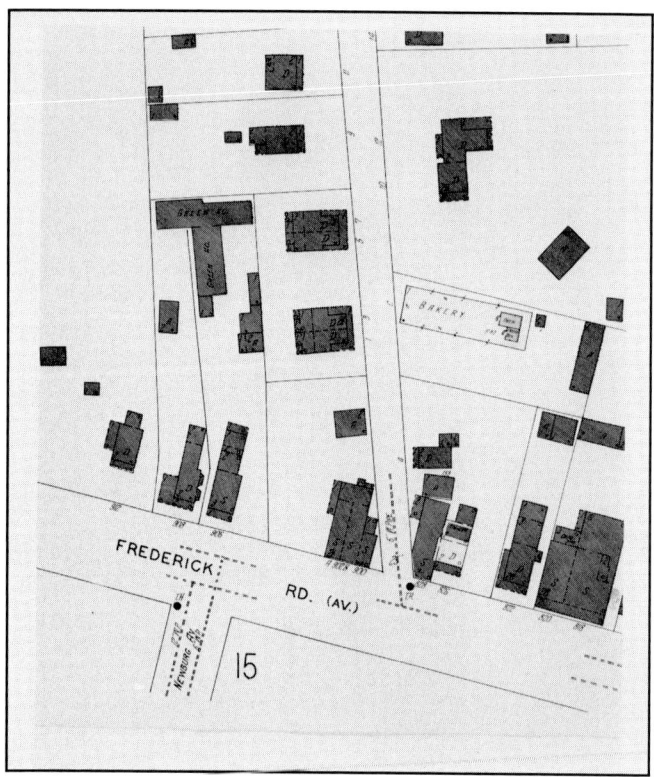

This detail from Map 9 shows the area surrounding the intersection of Frederick Road and Winters Lane. At 906 Frederick Road is the Harmon Flower Shop with its greenhouse in the rear. The large concrete block building was built in 1923 for Grim's Bakery.
Maryland Department, McKeldin Library, University of Maryland College Park

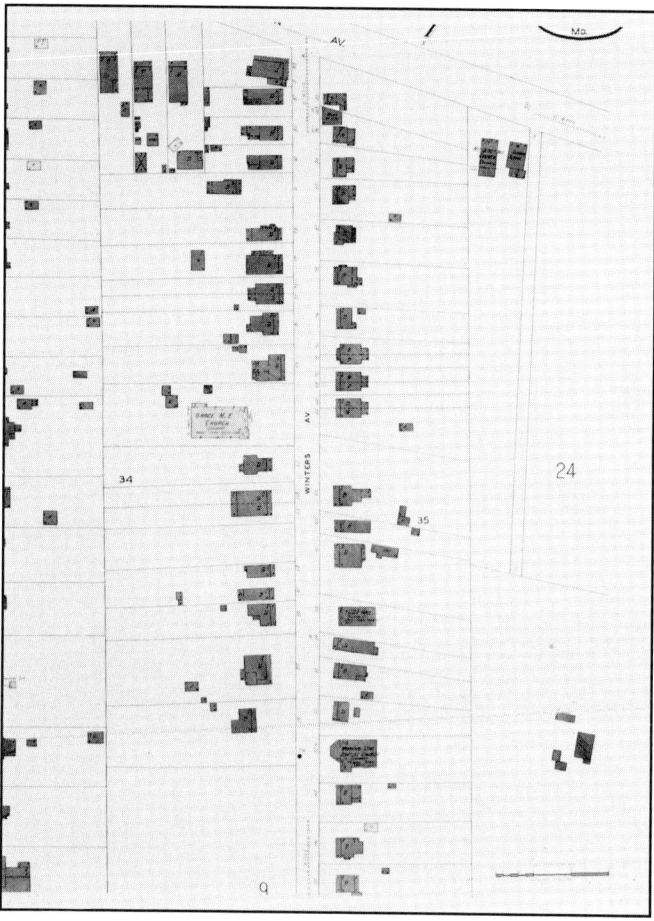

This detail from Map 8 shows Winters Lane, the center of Catonsville's black community. Four important community institutions can be seen: Morning Star Baptist Church, Odd Fellows Hall, Grace African Methodist Episcopal Church, and Mt. Olivet Methodist Church. Just beyond the area shown in this portion of the map, was the old colored school building that was bought by the the Full Gospel Tabernacle in 1943.
Maryland Department, McKeldin Library, University of Maryland College Park

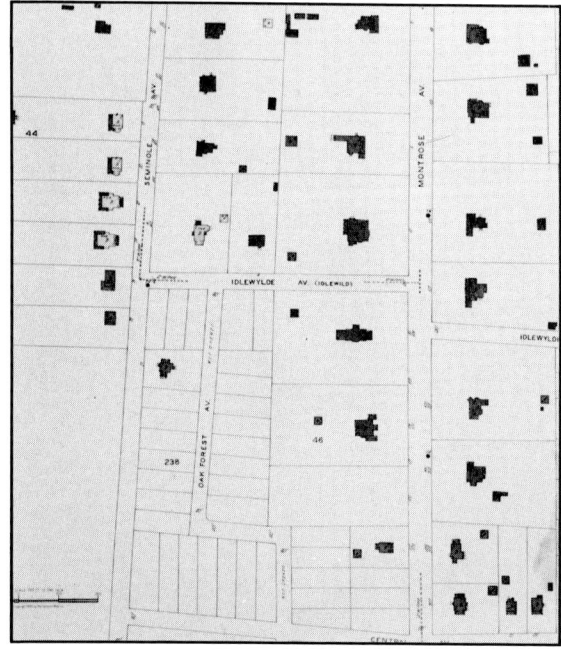

Map 22 illustrates the process of residential development in Oak Forest Park in the southwestern section of town. The large lots of Montrose Avenue are approximately one and one-half acres, while the lots in the lower right hand corner of the map—facing Central (now Ridge Road), Oak Forest and Seminole avenues—are approximately one-fifth acre.
Maryland Department, McKeldin Library, University of Maryland College Park

Catonsville Fire Insurance Maps, March 1930

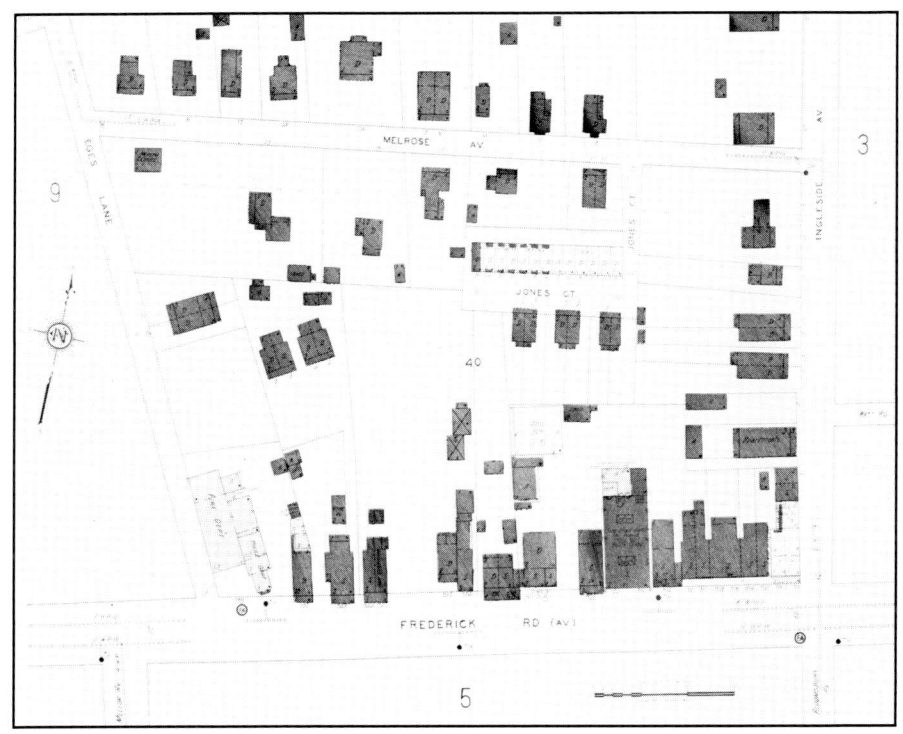

This detail from Map 2 shows the area on the north side of Frederick Road across from Wilson's Lumber Yard and the Alpha Theater. The old Railroad Hotel has been replaced by the County Fire and Police Station. The other notable new structure is Heidelbach's Grocery and Bakery, built in the mid 1920s.
Maryland Department, McKeldin Library, University of Maryland College Park

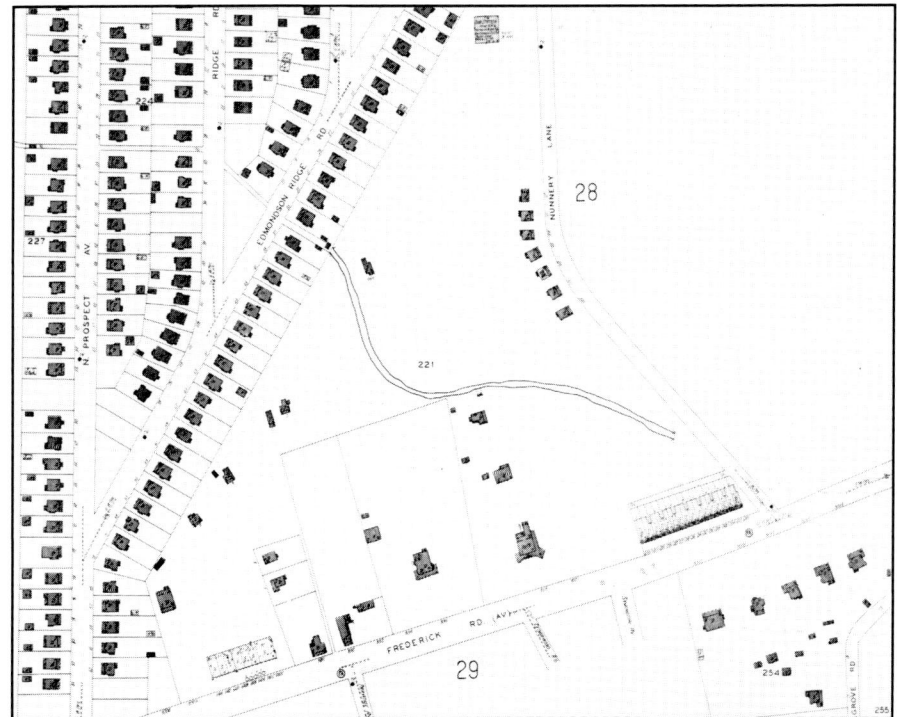

New bungalows line Prospect Avenue and Edmondson Ridge Road in the North Paradise section, developed during the 1920s on the east side of Catonsville. In the same decade, Mohler Brothers built a commercial row along the 6400 block of Frederick Road.
Maryland Department, McKeldin Library, University of Maryland College Park

The Village Center, 1920 to 1940

Looking east on Frederick Road at Ingleside Avenue in the 1920s. Prior to the installation of traffic lights, the policeman, shown on the left, would wheel his stop-and-go kiosk into the middle of the intersection where he would direct rush-hour traffic.
Jacques Kelly

The Village Center, 1920 to 1940

The old Catonsville Firehouse, built in 1887 at 22 Bloomsbury Avenue, served the county until 1928 and witnessed the transition from horse drawn vehicles to motorized units, shown here in 1915. It was remodeled and is still in existence for another purpose. In 1928 a new firehouse was built on the site of the old Railroad Hotel on Frederick Road and remains in use at the present time.
Catonsville Room

The No. 5 pumper truck at Catonsville's fire company, in the 1920s.
Jacques Kelly

The Village Center, 1920 to 1940

A service station with curbside gas pumps was housed at 918 Frederick Road in 1926. The building has had a remarkable variety of uses over the years, serving also as a grocery store (the early site of Heidelbach's), billiard parlor, movie house, bingo parlor, plumbing company, bank, and travel agency.
Catonsville Room

The Village Center, 1920 to 1940

The new Standard Oil Station at 612 Frederick Road was built in 1923 and featured drive-through service. It was remodeled and rebuilt through the years, but was razed in 1986 for a new office complex.
The Hughes Photo Company, Bafford Collection, Albin O. Kuhn Library, UMBC

We take pleasure in announcing the
OPENING
Thursday, March 1st, 1928
OF THE

ALPHA
Catonsville's Premier Motion Picture Theatre

Open to the Public at 6.30 P. M.

The attraction offered for our opening is United Artists' successful feature

"Sorrell and Son"

A picture for the entire family which will leave an abiding memory

Music by the "Kilgen Wonder Organ"
Mr. Stanley Boswell, Organist

ADMISSION: Adults, · · · 30 Cents
Children Under 12 Years, · 15 Cents

ELMER W. CASHMYER
ROBERT E. KANODE

PROGRAM:
   March 1-2, "Sorrell and Son"
   March 3, "In Old Kentucky"
   March 5-6, "Student Prince In Old Heidelberg"
   March 7, "Chang"
   March 8, "The Bugle Call"
   March 9-10, "The Big Parade"

Advertisement for the opening of the Alpha Theater in The Argus, February 25, 1928.

The Village Center, 1920 to 1940

The Alpha Theater as it appeared in the 1940s.
Catonsville Room

Frederick Road looking east from Newburg Avenue, 1935. Grim's Bakery can be seen on the far left.
Catonsville Room

Business Life in the 1920s and 1930s

Earl Dew in his newly opened Catonsville Sport Shop, 1940. Dew began business at 633 Frederick Road, near the corner of Bloomsbury, selling sporting goods and bicycles. His enterprise continued until 1978, when he retired.
Earl Dew

Construction by the Adamantex Brick Company, 1922. When Ashman's Department Store at 741 Frederick Road was severely damaged by fire, it was rebuilt and given this new brick facade. The new building included skylights, and Ashman advertised as "The Daylight Store." The structure later housed the Food Fair; today it is the site of the John S. Wilson Company. The photo was taken by the Hughes Photo Company.
Bafford Collection, Albin O. Kuhn Library, UMBC

Business Life in the 1920s and 1930s

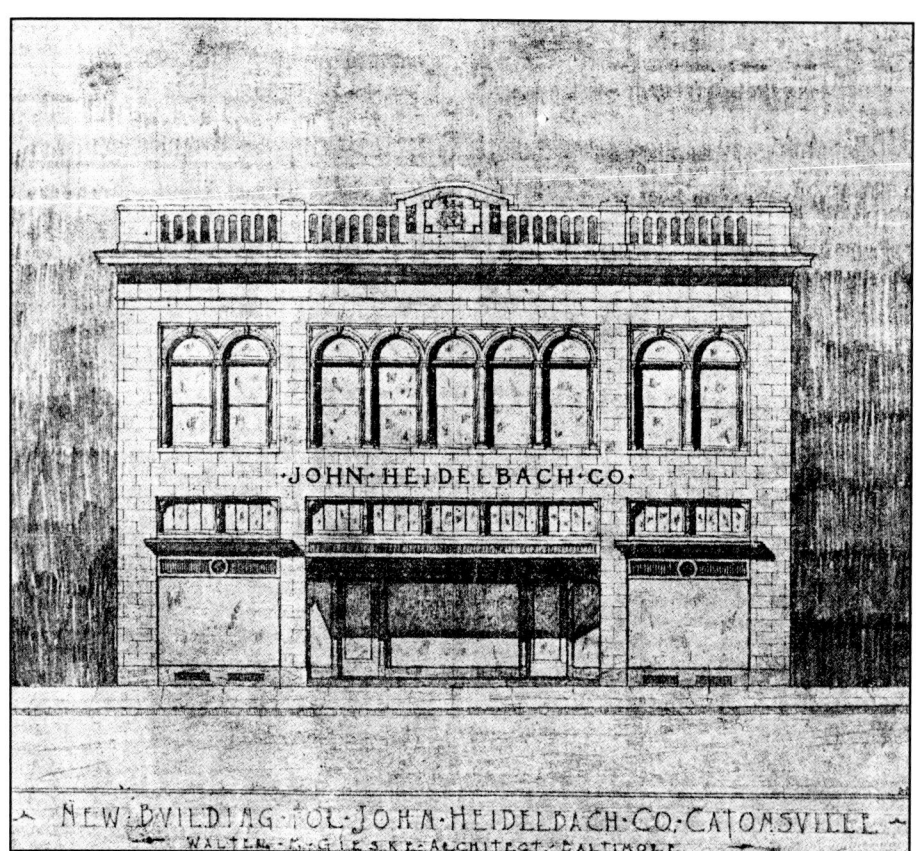

This sketch was published in The Argus in 1925 for the new quarters of the John Heidelbach company, 718-720 Frederick Road, next door to the grocery firm's previous location. The architect was local resident Walter Gieske, who designed many commercial and residential buildings. The new facility housed a bakery on the second floor. In the late 1920s Heidelbach's also opened a store in fashionable Roland Park.
Catonsville Room

John Heidelbach Company employees pose in 1934. The occasion was an outing for bakery workers. Pictured in the front row are the sons and widow of the firm's founder who continued to operate the business after his retirement in the 1920s; left to right are Walter, Sidney, Will, Mrs. John Heidelbach, George, and Ralph. The Catonsville store remained in business until 1965. The Roland Park store closed in 1978.
Catonsville Room

Advertisement in The Argus, April 17, 1926.

Business Life in the 1920s and 1930s

Delivery trucks for Harmon's Florist are parked near the greenhouses behind the shop, in the 1930s.
Ann Steffens

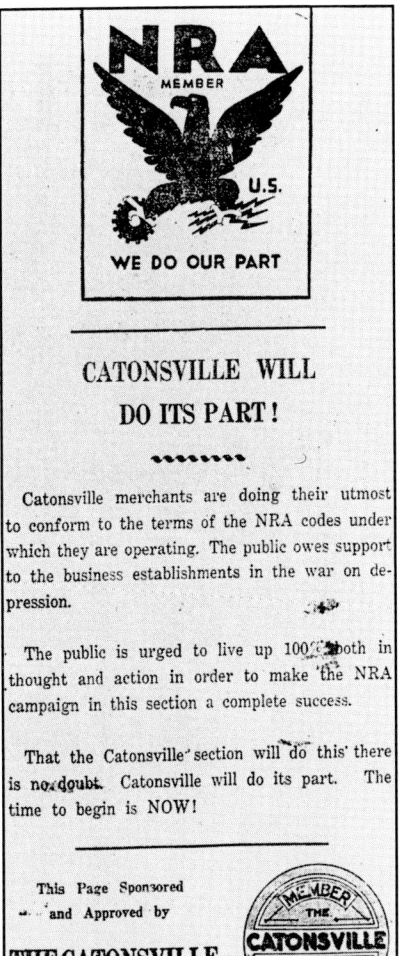

Catonsville merchants cooperated with New Deal administration efforts to help the country combat the Great Depression. Adherence to N.R.A. (National Recovery Act) codes was one measure of local support, as attested to by this 1933 Catonsville Board of Trade advertisement in the Catonsville Herald, *September 1, 1933.*

Building Homes in Catonsville: The Mohler Brothers

The Mohler brothers were not large scale builders like some in Baltimore City, but they were typical of the half dozen moderate-size developers active in Catonsville during the early decades of the twentieth century. Like most of the other Catonsville builders, they were local businessmen who lived in the community they were developing.

The Mohler family moved to Catonsville from Baltimore City shortly after the Baltimore Fire of 1904. Frank L. Mohler, Sr., was an executive with the E. J. Codd Company, marine engineers and architects, located in Fells Point. His spacious home in Catonsville, called Relhom (Mohler spelled backwards), later became the first Summit Nursing Home building in 1957, with a new structure replacing it in 1966. In this dwelling his nine children grew up. Three of them, Donald, Emile, and Frank, Jr., fought in World War I. After the war Donald and Emile went into the real estate and construction business.

The first major opportunity for the two young businessmen came in 1920 when they undertook the development of Summit, the James A. Gary estate. The property had been purchased in 1919 from the Gary family by Frank L. Mohler, Sr., Samuel D. Helfrich, and Martin Healy for $100,000. The Mohler brothers developed the land as a subdivision called Summit Park. Shortly thereafter, the Mohlers acquired a large piece of land fronting on Frederick Road west of Wade Avenue. This became the development of Holmehurst. In 1930 they began selling group homes in a development they named Somerset, located on Edmondson Avenue just west of Prospect Avenue.

The Great Depression halted the Mohlers' building activities in 1930. In 1937 they resumed construction but were forced to halt once again in 1941 when the United States entered World War II. However, by this time Mohler Brothers, Incorporated, had provided homes for almost two hundred families and created three of Catonsville's most attractive residential developments.

Building Homes in Catonsville: The Mohler Brothers

Donald I. Mohler with his wife, Dorothy Rigg Mohler and their children, Donald I., Jr., and John R., gather for a casual portrait in the rear yard of the home at 117 Forest Drive in Summit Park, 1929.
James W. Mohler

Emile R. Mohler pauses for the camera in the side yard of 6 Holmehurst Avenue, circa 1929.
James W. Mohler

Advertisement in The Argus, *May 15, 1920.*

The Mohler family, circa 1918. Standing in the back row are, left to right: Emile R. Mohler, Dorothy M. Mohler, Donald I. Mohler, and J. Edward Mohler. Seated in the front row are, left to right: Julia Virginia Mohler Waldron, Frank L. Mohler, Jr., Frank L. Mohler, Sr., John G. Mohler, Lily Brown Mohler, Gladys Joan Mohler Johnson, and Lily Brown Mohler Kirby. Donald and Emile, pictured in World War I era uniforms, later formed a partnership to build houses.
Catonsville Room

Summit Park

The sixty-four-acre estate of James A. Gary was developed by the Mohler Brothers as Summit Park. Their father had been one of the three purchasers of the land in 1919. The first sale of a lot reported in *The Argus* occurred in September, 1920. There were 156 lots in Summit Park, most of them slightly over one-third acre. An advertisement in June, 1921, called them "Home Sites of the Better Kind." The houses built in Summit Park ranged in size from large frame dwellings to small bungalows.

*An advertising brochure for Summit Park produced by the Mohler Brothers in 1922.
James W. Mohler*

*The outbuildings of the Gary mansion are shown on this 1922 map of lots in Summit Park (on lots C-2, D-8, and D-11). They were removed by 1927.
James W. Mohler*

Summit Park

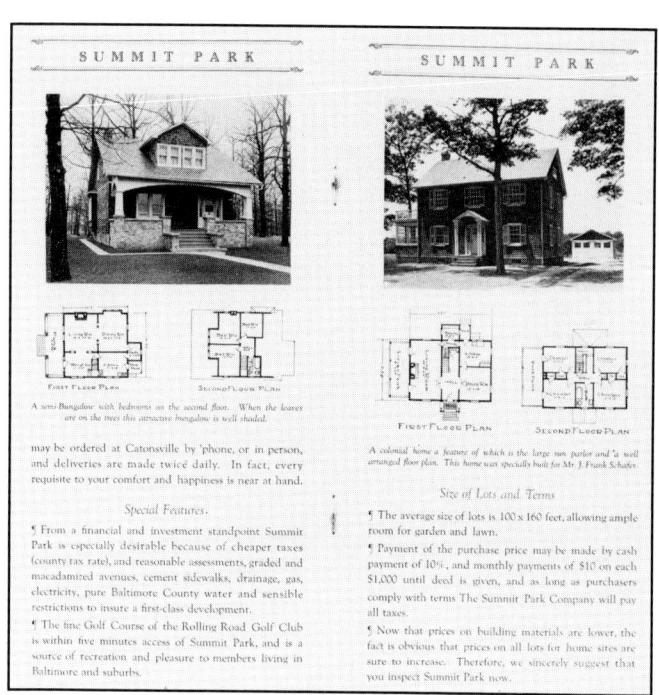
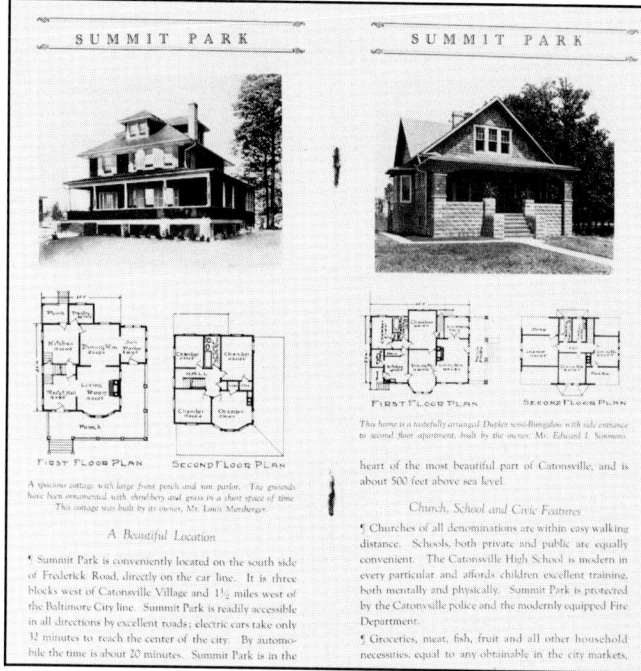

Summit Park advertising brochure, 1922.
James W. Mohler.

Advertisement for apartments in the former Gary mansion in The Argus, *September 15, 1923.*

Summit Park

The home of Donald I. Mohler at 117 Forest Drive was built in 1923. James W. Mohler

Advertisement in The Argus, *June 18, 1921.*

SUMMIT PARK

CATONSVILLE

On Frederick Road and Car Line
—Two Squares West of Village

Home-sites of the BETTER KIND are now available in this established suburb, where all the surroundings are beautified by very attractive homes.

This suburb has natural shade trees and lawns, macadam avenues, cement sidewalks, county water, sewerage, gas, electricity and county tax rate. One of the greatest advantages of this location is that it is in a fine neighborhood and only two squares from all churches, schools, stores, etc. Carefully restricted.

MOHLER BROTHERS

713 AMERICAN BUILDING

Office
St. Paul 3857

Residence
Catons 189-J

Holmehurst

In 1922 the Mohler Brothers acquired twenty-two acres fronting on Frederick Road. They divided the area into sixty lots which were approximately one-third of an acre each, slightly smaller than the Summit Park lots. They began building homes in the development in 1923. They were forced to stop construction in 1930 due to the Great Depression, but managed to erect two houses in 1936. Between 1938 and 1940 they built nineteen more houses, indicating that the economic depression had lifted considerably in the local area by the late 1930s.

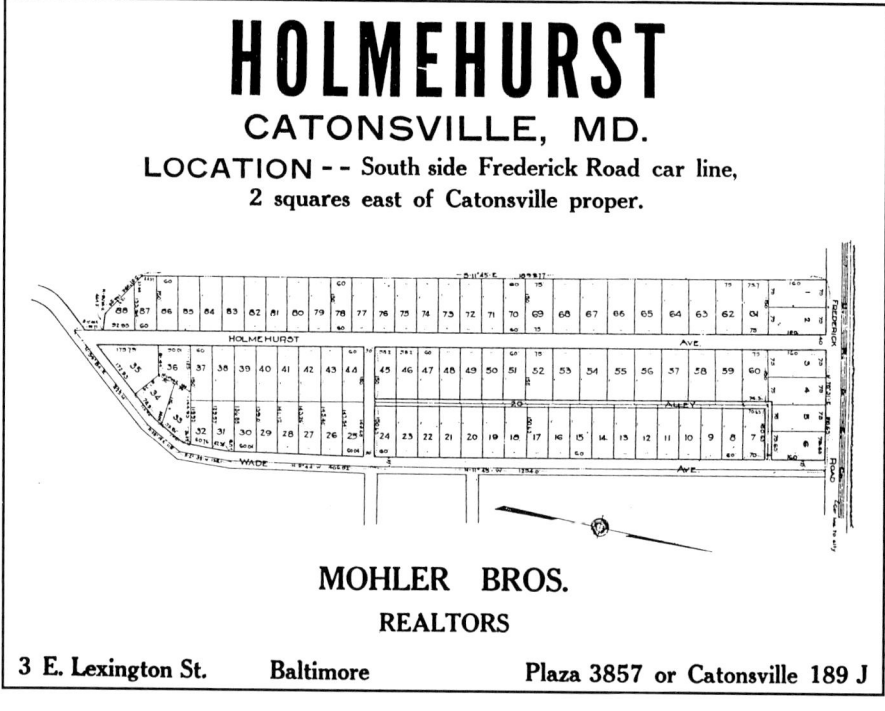

Map showing lots for Holmehurst development, circa 1923.
James W. Mohler

A new house at 11 Holmehurst Avenue, circa 1929.
James W. Mohler

Holmehurst

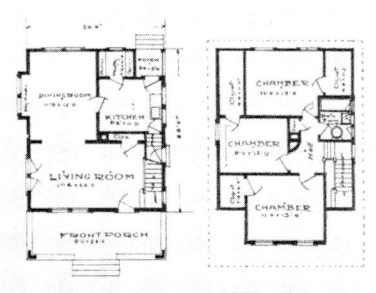

HOLMEHURST-CATONSVILLE
OPPOSITE EDEN TERRACE

WE WANT YOU TO INSPECT AND COMPARE THIS HOME **$5700.** Get off No. 8 Car at Frederick Road and Wade Avenue

Holmehurst is located on Frederick Road Carline, just two squares east of Catonsville's 48 stores, 10 churches and 8 schools. Eden Terrace, directly opposite, is a community of beautiful homes, assuring you of the best surroundings.

WHY EVER PAY RENT? WHEN LOW TERMS BUYS ALL THIS:

1st. A well selected location. A home built by Mohler Bros., embraces everything a person desires. 6 spacious rooms, pantry, bath, 4 big cupboards. A home built high and dry on a lot 60x150 feet.

2nd. Within one square of Catonsville car line. 30 minutes to center of city.

3rd. County taxes—very much less than City taxes.

4th. Designed with home comforts in view—at same time, very attractive.

5th. Macadam avenues with cement sidewalks already installed.

6th. Ornamental shrubbery planted between walks and avenues.

7th. City water, gas and electricity already installed.

8th. Hard surfaced alley for garages and tradesmen.

9th. Pipeless Furnace furnished—we will give choice of other heating plants at cost.

10th. One piece apron front, white enamel sink and very good gas range.

11th. Painting—good quality paint used and attractive color schemes.

12th. Plenty of electric sockets throughout house. One in kitchen for electric iron.

13th. Best quality window frames and sash are used—namely, white pine and cypress.

14th. Large air chambers over second floor rooms.

15th. Cement laundry tubs in basement.

16th. 30 gallon water boiler, connected with heating plant and gas water heater.

17th. Well lighted stairway.

18th. Medicine cabinet with windows, one on each side.

19th. Special electric fixtures used.

20th. Entrance to cellar is on side of house, which is more useful and attractive than old style entrances and keeps out snow and rain.

21st. Large bright dining room with bay window.

22nd. Reasonable ground rent.

23rd. Liberal terms given.

24th. We will also build according to your plans.

Call Plaza 3857 and we will call for you.

LOTS AND COTTAGES

MOHLER BROTHERS REALTORS
3 East LEXINGTON Street
Baltimore, Md.

HOME PHONES
CATONSVILLE
705 AND 189-J

Advertising broadside, circa 1924.
James W. Mohler

The Mohler Brothers ledger book shows construction expenses for 24 Holmehurst Avenue during November and December, 1938.
James W. Mohler

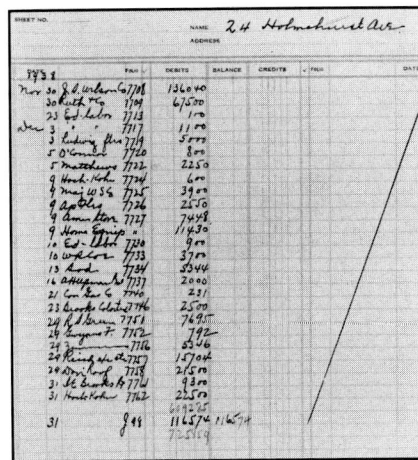

145

Somerset Group Homes

The Somerset homes development was begun in 1930 on the south side of Edmondson Avenue just down the hill from Mt. de Sales Academy, a well-known Roman Catholic school for girls. The first group of six houses varied in price from $6,250 to $6,750. They were a refreshing architectural departure from the typical Baltimore row house and were praised by the Baltimore *Sun* for the high quality of their design. All the units were quickly sold to young newly-married couples and were known locally as "brides row." The Mohler Brothers built this development under the name Edmondson Avenue Homes, Incorporated.

Somerset group homes are shown with Edmondson Avenue streetcar tracks in the foreground, 1930. Today these homes are 1 through 6 Somerset Road, the small frontage road on which the automobiles are parked.
James W. Mohler

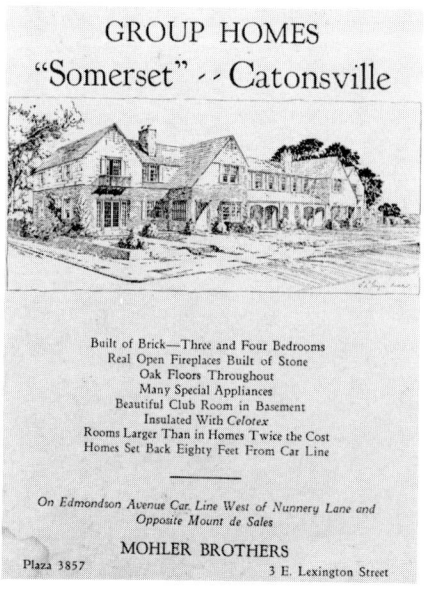

Advertising broadside, 1930.
James W. Mohler

Catonsville's Churches

Grace African Methodist Episcopal Church at 67 ½ Winters Lane, 1912, was rebuilt on the site of an earlier wooden structure, which had been destroyed by fire in 1911.
Mae Esther Coe

St. Mark Catholic Church on Melvin Avenue, shown here probably in the early 1920s, was built in 1888. It now serves as the parish chapel.
Hughes Photo Company; Bafford Collection, Albin O. Kuhn Library, UMBC

Catonsville's Churches

Catonsville's Churches

Laying of the cornerstone ceremonies are celebrated for the new facilities of the Catonsville Methodist Episcopal Church at 6 Melvin Avenue, June 28, 1924. Melvin Avenue is on the right; in the background is the parsonage and behind it is the earlier church, its tower visible. The older church structure had been dedicated in 1887 at the corner of Frederick and Melvin. The photo was made by the Hughes Photo Company of Baltimore, using a special panoramic camera.
Bafford Collection,
Albin O. Kuhn Library, UMBC

The Women's Civic Club campaigned for a new school building for Catonsville's black youth, citing the old structure's lack of toilets and plumbing facilities, leaky ceiling, and fire hazards. The new school, constructed in 1923 with four rooms (others were added later), was subsequently named for Benjamin Banneker (1731-1806), considered the first American black man of science, whose farm was on Old Frederick Road at Oella Avenue, a site now being developed by Baltimore County as the Benjamin Banneker Historical Park.

The following realty note appeared in *The Argus*, January 27, 1923:

Contract for Colored School at Catonsville Awarded

Baltimore County Board of Education has awarded the contract for erecting a new colored school house at Catonsville to Hicks & Son for $34,910. It will be an eight room building. The school was urged by the Women's Civic League of Catonsville.

A second new school building was constructed in the 1920s, this one for a growing white population. Catonsville High School, shown here in 1928, opened in 1925 on the site of the old Catonsville Country Club.
Catonsville Room

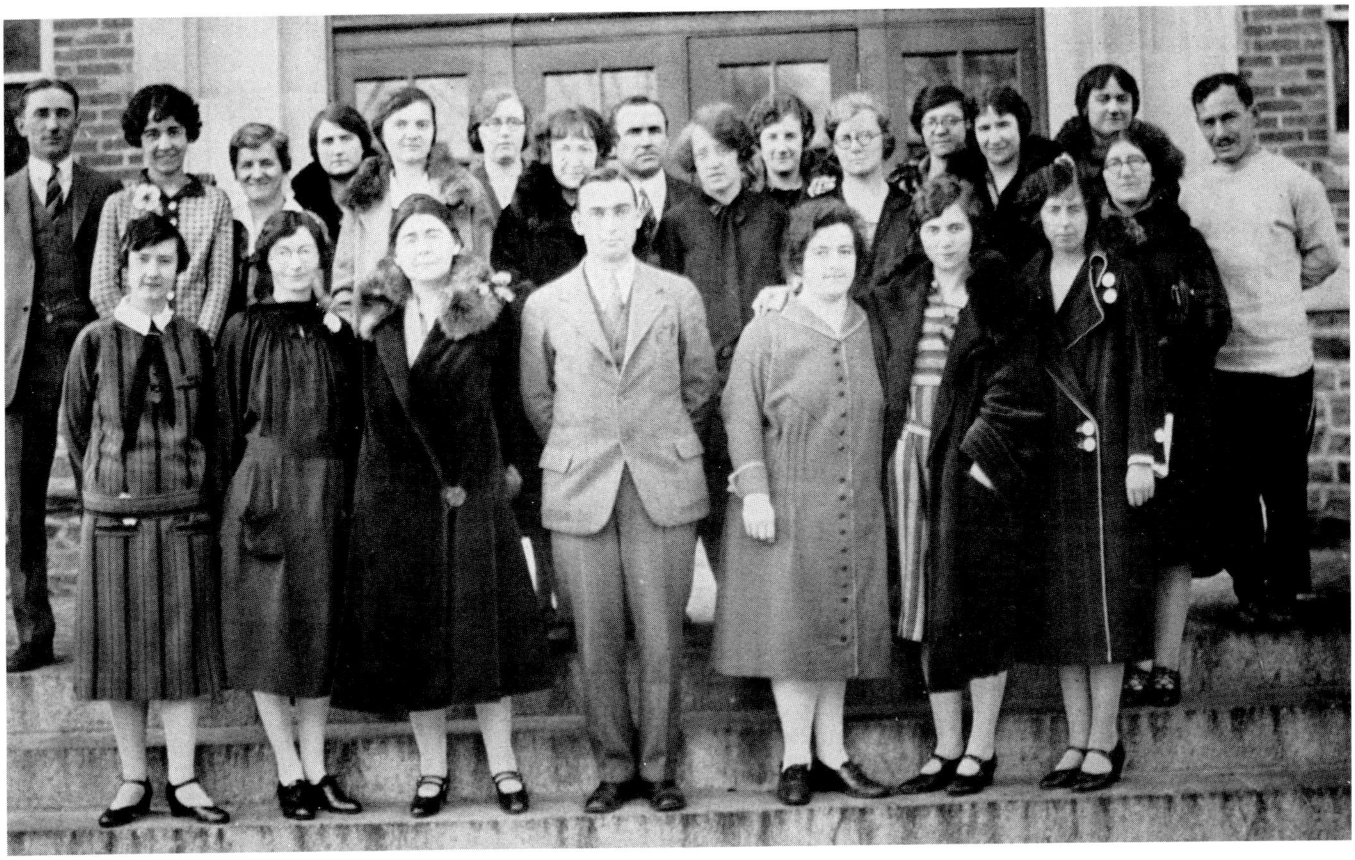

The Catonsville High School faculty of 1927 had grown from the 1914 faculty of only eight persons. The June Bug, 1927. Catonsville Room

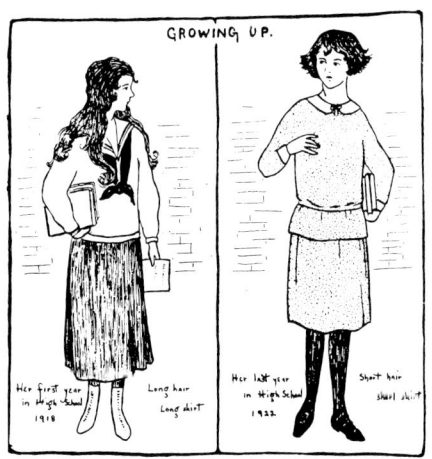

"Growing Up," appeared in the Catonsville High School Yearbook, The June Bug, in 1922.
Catonsville Room

OUR FORDS

Just look at our Fords,
Ramshackle and rough.
Bolts missing, no brakes,
And more than one scuff.

This runabout here,
Fred just acquired.
It's tires are all flat.
And its doors have been wired.

See this shining one?
Sam, as its master,
Says the din of its rattles
Makes it go faster.

Elmer's is muddy
'Cause it came a long way
It's cold, so a blanket
Keeps it warm all day.

This one, be-curtained,
Was brought in by Bill.
Tho balky at mountains
Will coast down a hill.

Now these two coupes
With windows so clean (?)
Each morning and lunch hour
Bring Mac and Boze to the scene.

But despite all they lack.
The times that they stall.
And the gas that they waste.
Our Fords are loved by all.

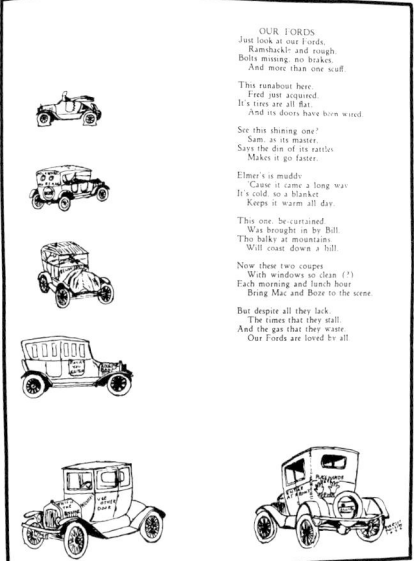

The poem "Our Fords," was printed in The June Bug in 1926.
Catonsville Room

High School Life

Catonsville High School girls basketball team, 1934.
Catonsville Room

High School Life

Graduates from Mt. de Sales Academy in 1922, top row, left to right, are: Mary Parish, Mary Wilkinson, and Mary Condry. Bottom row, left to right, are: Josephine Harmon, Victorine Peach, Annette Hampson, Alice Haynes, and Charlotte Lamble.
Ann Steffens

Life in Boom Time and Hard Times

Members of the Ladies' Aid Society, Salem Lutheran Church, picnic at the Magothy River in 1937. Pictured, left to right are: Esther Reich, Louise Freund, Lena Werner, Emily Wagner, and Adelaide Bowers (wife of the pastor, John G. Bowers).
Catonsville Room

Life in Boom Times and Hard Times

The Crescent Elks Baseball Team, shown here in the 1930s, played its games at Suter Field, near Winters Lane.
Mae Esther Coe

Edward and Mildred Maisel, in the early 1920s.
Dorothy Maisel Reis

Life in Boom Times and Hard Times

This 1923 children's party photo, from the Hughes Company Collection, is listed as having been taken for Mrs. E. L. Pittroff of Catonsville.
Bafford Collection, Albin O. Kuhn Library, UMBC

Life in Boom Time and Hard Times

"Gossip Bench" visitors outside Kalb's Pottery at 802 Frederick Road in 1929 are, left to right, John Ammenhauser, George Boston, and F. C. Raab, Jr. This spot, comfortably close to the warmth of the pottery kilns in the winter, long was a popular gathering place for some of the community's men.
Catonsville Room

Life in Boom Times and Hard Times

The Harmonie Singing Society performs at the laying of the cornerstone of a new building for the General German Orphan Asylum on Bloomsbury Avenue, July 6, 1922. The institution is now named the Children's Home.
Jacques Kelly

Life in Boom Times and Hard Times

*Rolling Road Golf Club, circa 1930.
Jacques Kelly*

A Frederick Road Family: The Harmons

The family of John B. Harmon, Jr., exemplifies the transition of Catonsville from village to suburb. John B. Harmon, Sr., orginally joined the Catonsville community as an overseer on the D. C. Howell estate, Belle Grove, which was located on Frederick Road at what is now Belle Grove Road. As the village of Catonsville changed into a busy suburban community, the Harmons became entrepreneurs—first as dry goods merchants and then as florists at 906 Frederick Road where the family business continued until 1966.

A family portrait of John Harmon, Jr., and his sisters in the 1910s; left to right are: Isabel, Margaret, Agnes (seated), John, Jr., and Josephine.
Ann Steffens

A Frederick Road Family: The Harmons

John B. Harmon, Sr. (1862-1927), poses with his children outside his home at Belle Grove, where he worked as a caretaker until 1911.
Ann Steffens

John's mother, Mary Agnes Harmon (1862-1945), poses for a photograph in front of "M. A. Harmon, Stationers," the dry goods store at 906 Frederick Road, purchased by the Harmon family in 1911.
Ann Steffens

John B. Harmon, Jr., is pictured at about age seven, presumably at the time of his First Holy Communion at St. Mark Catholic Church, where he attended the parochial school.
Ann Steffens

A Frederick Road Family: The Harmons

In a 1913 photo, Mary Agnes Harmon (left) displays the sundry wares sold at the Frederick Road store.
Ann Steffens

In 1914, Mrs. Harmon shifted the dry goods to one side of the shop when her husband transferred the talents he had used at Belle Grove to open a florist shop on the other side of the premises. Pictured are the Harmon family members preparing for their first Easter as florists.
Ann Steffens

A Frederick Road Family: The Harmons

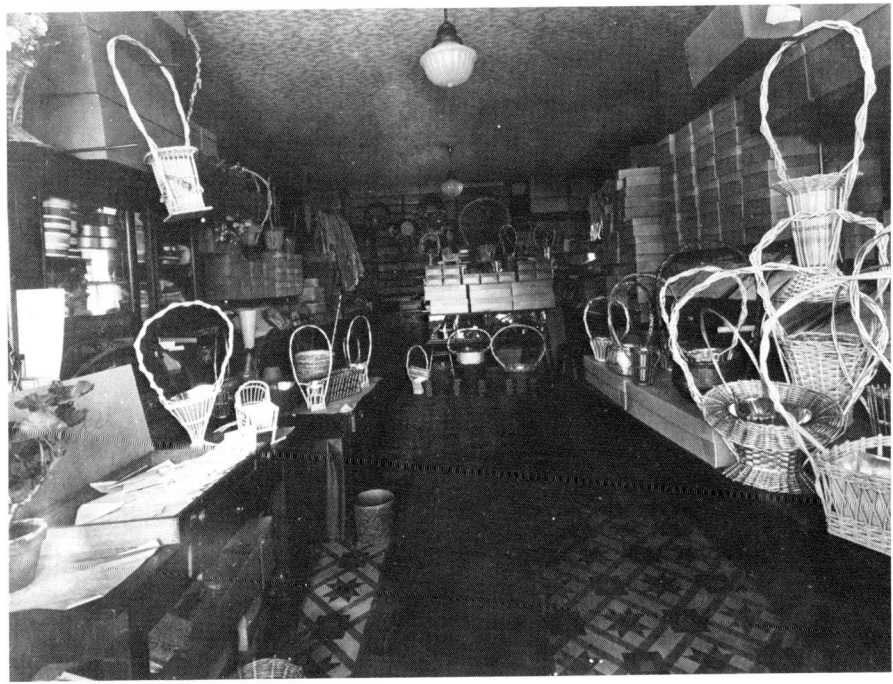

Eventually the florist shop took over the entire space at the Frederick Road address. The greenhouse in the rear had been moved from the estate of Frank Brown, who served as Maryland governor, 1892 to 1896. This building was also expanded as the Harmon business prospered.
Ann Steffens

A Frederick Road Family: The Harmons

John, Jr., graduated from Mt. St. Joseph's College High School. At age nineteen he entered the army to fight in World War I, but did not forget the family's close association with the florist business. In a letter from "Somewhere in France," dated November 7, 1917, John wrote to his father of "some of the most beautiful outside chrysanthemums and dahlias that could be raised." He returned home safely in 1918.
Ann Steffens

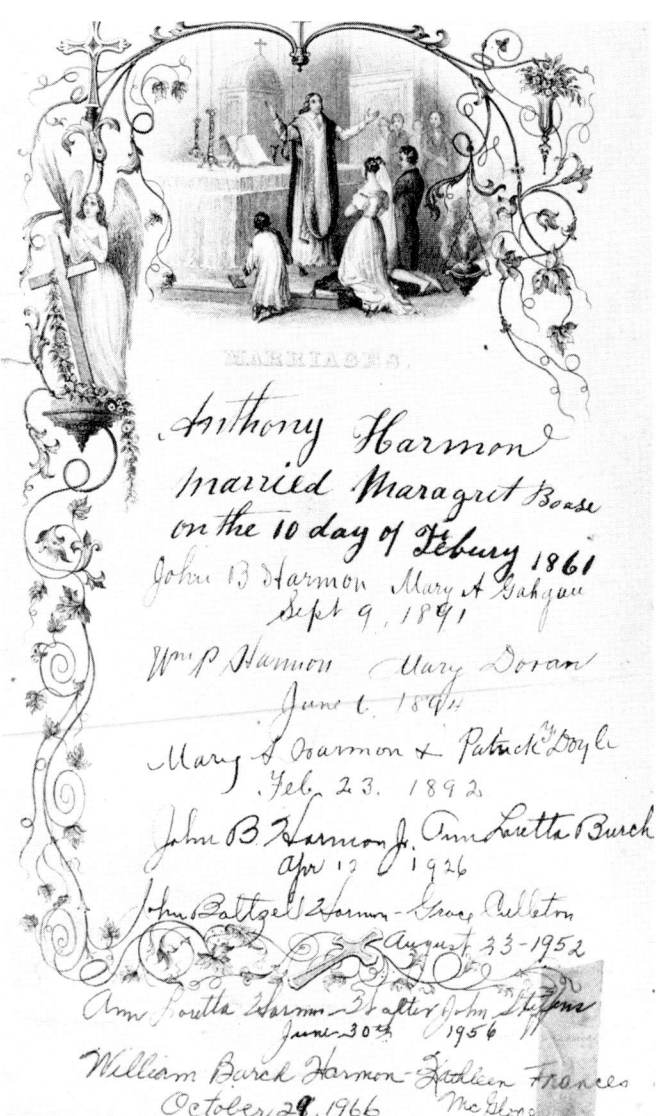

A page from the Harmon family Bible records the marriages of John, Sr., to Mary Agnes Gahgan (1891), and of John, Jr., to Ann Loretta Burch (1926), as well as the marriages of two of their children who have resided in Catonsville: Ann Loretta Harmon to Walter John Steffens (1956); and William Burch Harmon to Kathleen Frances McGlone (1966).
Ann Steffens and Burch Harmon

A Frederick Road Family: The Harmons

On April 12, 1926, John B. Harmon, Jr., married Ann Loretta Burch at Sts. Philip and James Catholic Church in Baltimore. Susan Burch, sister of the bride, was maid of honor, and Leo C. Read, of Eden Terrace, was best man.
Ann Steffens and Burch Harmon

When John B. Harmon, Sr., died in 1927, his wife and his two sisters, Margaret and Josephine, continued the family business. Pictured is George Cavey, of Fusting Avenue, loading the truck for delivery in 1935.

John, Jr., joined the florist shop in 1943, after a career as a manufacturer's representative, remaining there until his death in 1960. His sisters then maintained the business until 1966, when it was sold to the present owners, Mr. and Mrs. Howard Medicus, who continue to operate the shop under the name of Hilton Florist.
Ann Steffens and Burch Harmon

*A community tradition since 1947, Catonsville's Fourth of July Parade in 1953 attracted large crowds, who watched the marchers turn down Bloomsbury Avenue from Frederick Road in front of the building formerly called the Old Corner Store, a reminder of village days, by then a sales outlet for a national manufacturer, and now an office for O'Conor, Piper and Flynn Realtors.
Catonsville Room*

Chapter VI

Beyond 1940

World War II took dozens of the community's young people to serve in the armed forces. The wartime era also brought full employment to Catonsville and a tremendous economic boom to the entire Baltimore region, but the recently revived home construction industry ground to a complete halt because of wartime restrictions on materials.

When the great conflict finally ended in 1945, few in Catonsville imagined the degree to which the postwar population explosion in the Baltimore region would transform their village. One by one the remaining lots within the village were filled with new houses. Outside the community, fields and farms were covered by construction projects of a size never before seen in the locality: shopping centers, huge housing projects, businesses, and educational institutions spread across hundreds of acres. Frederick Road was superseded by the four-lane divided highway called the Baltimore National Pike, built one mile north of the town. This new thoroughfare was soon lined with shopping centers, auto dealerships, discount stores, and supermarkets, all of which cut deeply into the sales of the old Frederick Road shops. In 1955 the Maryland State Highway Commission took a wide swath from the eastern section of Catonsville for the new Baltimore Beltway—destroying a number of Eden Terrace's most attractive homes. The beltway became the main artery for the county's suburban transformation, tying Catonsville even more closely to the growing metropolitan region.

By the 1980s the suburban fringe had passed

Beyond 1940

beyond Catonsville. The town was now completely surrounded by houses, shopping centers, highways, and large-scale institutions like the new campuses of the University of Maryland Baltimore County and Catonsville Community College. While Catonsville was surrounded, it was not overrun. In fact, the new highways and large-scale developments appear to have established fairly clear boundaries for the community without destroying its fundamental structure or form. Thus, at the end of the 1980s Catonsville remains a distinct community within the sprawling suburban hinterland of Baltimore County, its character rooted, at least in part, in its village past.

The last streetcar makes its way west along Frederick Road, November 2, 1963. Catonsville Room

Beyond 1940

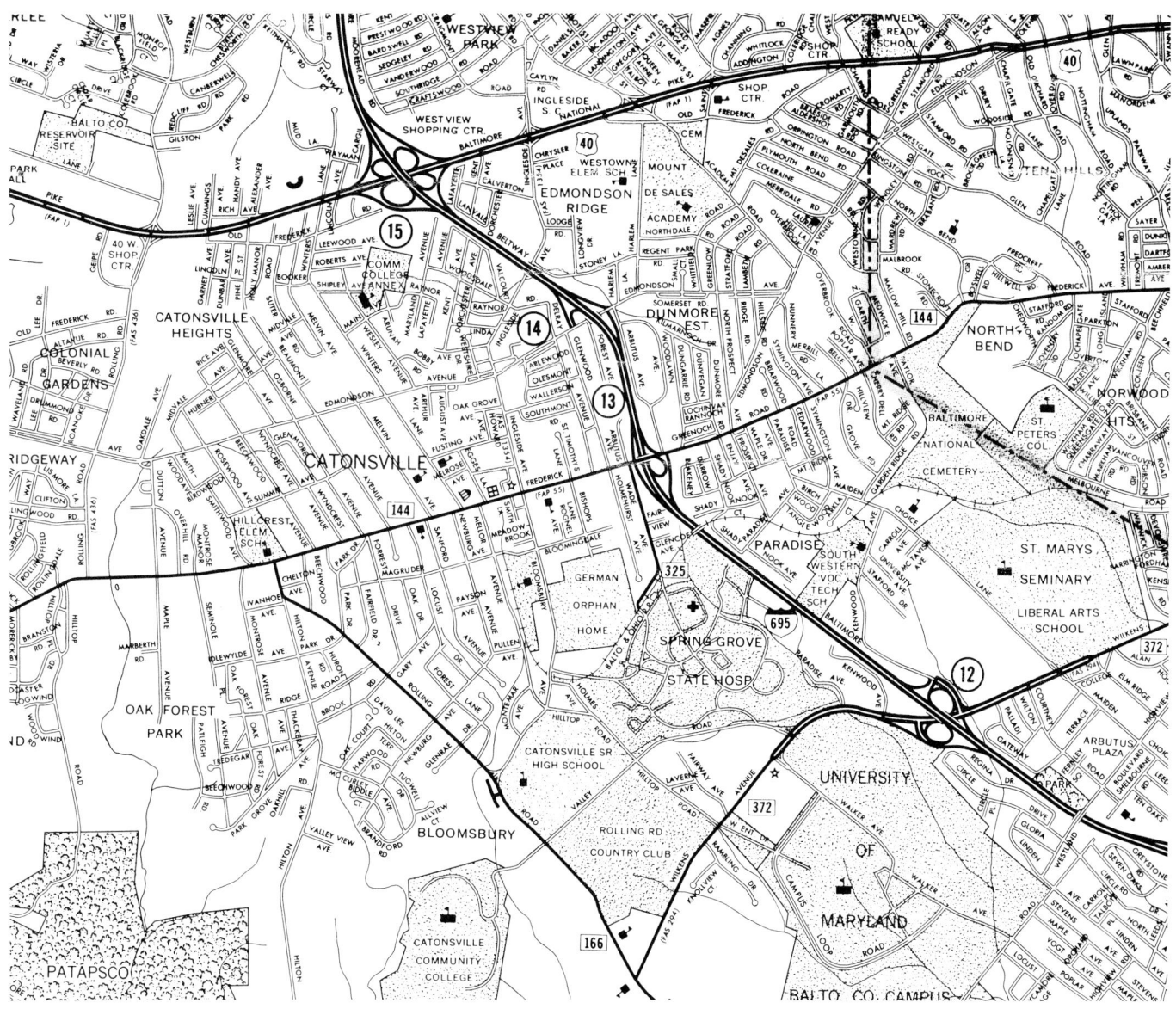

Map of Catonsville, 1972
Maryland Department of Transportation,
State Highway Administration, Baltimore
Washington Metropolitan Area Map
Series, Map No. 22 (1972)

Bibliography

Bedini, Silvio A. *The Life of Benjamin Banneker.* New York: Charles Scribners' Sons, 1972.

Bromley, George W. and Walters, S. *Atlas of Baltimore County, Maryland.* Baltimore: G.W. Bromley & Company, 1898.

Brooks, Neal A. and Parsons, Richard. *Baltimore County Panorama.* Towson, Maryland: Baltimore County Library, 1988.

Brooks, Neal A. and Rockel, Eric G. *A History of Baltimore County.* Towson, Maryland: Friends of the Towson Library, 1979.

Farrell, Michael R. *Who Made All Our Streetcars Go? The Story of Rail Transit in Baltimore.* Baltimore: NRHS Publications, 1973.

Gontrum, Edwin K., ed. *Sidelights on the History of Baltimore County.* Towson, Maryland: by the author, 1966.

Heidelbach, Ralph H. *Catonsville in the Round Before 1918.* Catonsville, Maryland: by the author, 1988.

Heidelbach, Ralph H. *Village of Catonsville: Historical Background, 1890-1915.* Catonsville, Maryland: by the author, 1987.

Hollifield, William. *Difficulties Made Easy: A History of the Turnpikes of Baltimore City and County.* Towson, Maryland: Baltimore County Historical Society, 1978.

Hopkins, G. M. Company, *Atlas of Baltimore County, Maryland.* Baltimore: G. M. Hopkins Company, 1877.

Keidel, George C. *Colonial History of Catonsville: Bicentennial Edition.* Catonsville, Maryland: American Bicentennial Committee of Catonsville, 1976.

Maples, Robert L. *Highlights in the History of Catonsville.* Catonsville, Maryland: by the author, 1972.

Marks, Bayly Ellen, *Hilton Heritage.* Catonsville, Maryland: Catonsville Community College, 1972.

McGrain, John W. *Grist Mills in Baltimore County, Maryland.* Towson, Maryland: Baltimore County Library, 1980.

Perkins, D. B. *Picturesque Catonsville.* n. p. 1895.

Sanborn Map Company, *Sanborn Fire Insurance Map of Catonsville, Maryland, 1910.* New York: Sanborn Map Company, 1910.

Sanborn Map Company, *Sanborn Fire Insurance Map of Catonsville, Maryland, 1925.* New York: Sanborn Map Company, 1925.

Sanborn Map Company, *Sanborn Fire Insurance Map of Catonsville, Maryland, 1930.* New York: Sanborn Map Company, 1930.

Scharf, J. Thomas. *History of Baltimore City and County from the Earliest Period to the Present Day.* Philadelphia: Louis H. Evarts, 1881.

Index

A

Adamantex Brick Company, 135
Alpha Theater, 124, 127, 129, 133-134
Ammenhauser, John, 157
Annexation, Baltimore City, 1918, 62, 124
Arden (residence), 39
The Argus, 6, 21, 24, 36, 61-62, 124
Ashman's Department Store, 135

B

Baker, Bernard, 116
Ball family estate, 90
Baltimore National Pike, 167
Banneker, Benjamin, 150
Banneker School, 150
Belle Grove (residence), 27, 160-162
Beltway, through Catonsville, 39, 124, 167
Bion, Elsie, 45
Bloede, Carl, 41
Bloede, Victor G., and family, 21, 38-39, 41, 44
Bloomsbury (residence), 54, 59
Blue and Gold, 108
Bockmiller, Richard B. and Elizabeth, and family, 106
Boston, George, 157
Boston, Thomas H. and Elizabeth, and family, 25, 93, 117-121
Bowers, Adelaide, 154
Brink, Charles, 44
Brink house (residence), 44, 51
Burch, Ann Loretta (Harmon), 165
Burch, Susan, 165

C

Carozza, Anthony, 116
Carroll, Charles (of Carrollton), 15
Castle Thunder, 10-11
Caton, Richard, 10-11, 15
Caton Spring Company, 39
Catonsville Baseball Club, 112
Catonsville Casino (country club), 46
Catonsville Christadelphian Church, 12
Catonsville Colored Elementary School, 62, 107, 111, 120-121, 124, 128, 150
Catonsville Community College, 12, 168
Catonsville Country Club, 46, 126
Catonsville Elementary School, 48, 91, 107, 111
Catonsville Herald, 124
Catonsville High School, 12, 46, 59, 61, 106-111, 124, 126, 150-152
Catonsville Hotel, 36, 108, 126
Catonsville Improvement Company, 105
Catonsville Junction, 122
Catonsville Methodist Episcopal Church, 12, 149
Catonsville Presbyterian Church, 12
Catonsville Short Line Railroad, 12-13, 17, 20-21, 24, 30, 38
Catonsville Short Line Railroad Depot, 30, 35, 124, 127
Cavey, George, 165
Chamberlain, Jesse, 114
Coe, Edgar Alexander, 111, 120-121
Coe, Mae Esther, 120-121
Coe, Livous and Annie (Boston), and family, 13, 117-121
Condry, Mary, 153
Crescent Elks Baseball team, 155

D

Dew, Earl, Sporting Goods and Bicycle Shop, 135
Diehlmann, Christian and Daniel, 114
Dorsey, Hammond, 56

E

Eden Construction Company, 39
Eden Terrace, 13, 21, 38-45, 51, 124, 167
Eigenbrot's Beer, 12-13
Ellicott City (Ellicott's Mills), 15, 24, 105

F

Farmlands (residence) 12, 53, 55-59
Firehouse, Catonsville, 12, 35, 129, 131
First National Bank of Catonsville, 31, 61, 96, 115
Forest Spring Park, 61, 105
Forster, Will, and family, 41, 45
Franklintown, 17
Frederick Douglass High School (Baltimore), 111, 120
Frederick Road (views of), 94-97, 130, 134, 166
Frederick Turnpike, 11-12, 15-16
Freund, Louise, 154
Full Gospel Tabernacle, 128
Fusting, Charles, 34
Fusting, Joseph P., 11, 18, 34

G

Gary, James A., 28, 138, 140
General German Orphan Home, 158
Gerwig, John, homebuilder, 13, 106, 141
Gieske, Gustav, 29
Gieske, Walter, 136
Goldstein, Samuel R. ("Sam the Tailor"), and family, 98-99
Gray Gables (residence), 41, 45
Grace African Methodist Episcopal Church, 12, 118, 128, 147
Grim's Bakery, 12, 128, 134
Grim's Flour, Feed, and Country Produce Store, 100

H

Hall, H. P., 42
Hampson, Annette, 153
Harmon, John B., Jr., and Ann Loretta, and family, 91, 160-161, 164-165
Harmon, John B., Sr., and Mary Agnes, and family, 13, 102-103, 160-165
Harmon, Burch, 169

Harmon, Josephine, 153
Harmon, Kathleen Frances (McGlone), 164
Harmonie Singing Society, 158
Harmon's Flower Shop, 102-103, 128, 137, 161-165
Haynes, Alice, 153
Healy, Martin, 138
Heidelbach, William J., and family, 99, 136
Heidelbach's Grocery Store (Frederick Road), 12, 99, 129, 132, 136
Heidelbach's Grocery Store (Roland Park), 136
Heinmuller family, 86
Helfrich, Samuel D., 138
Hilton (residence), 12
Hilton Florist, 165
Hoffman, William S., blacksmith, 33
Holloway, J. W., 104
Holmehurst, 138-139, 144-145
Home-ownership, Catonsville, 1910, 92
Homewood (residence), 18
Horsecar line, 16, 24, 37, 60
Howell, D. C., 27, 160
Hubner, John, 13, 105
Hunting Ridge (early name for area), 12

I

Ingleside (residence), 116
Irvington, 16

J

Jones, Edith, Florence and Julia, 47
June Bug, 110, 151

K

Kalb's Pottery Shop, 157
Keidel, Henry, 18

L

Lamble, Charlotte, 153

Lentz, Frederick and family, 87
Library, Baltimore County, Catonsville Area Branch, 10
Library Hall, 24, 30-31, 101, 125
Loudon Park Cemetery, 16
Lurman, Frances, 53-55, 59
Lurman, Gustav, W., Jr., and Elizabeth, and family, 52-59
Lurman, Gustav, Sr., and Frances Donnell, and family, 13, 53, 56, 58-59
Lurman, Theodor, 53, 58

M

Maisel, Edward and Mildred, 155
Maisel, Frederick, Jr., homebuilder, 13, 106
Map, Catonsville (G. M. Hopkins, 1877), 19
Map, Catonsville (Bromley, 1898), 22, 38, 105
Map, Catonsville (Maryland State Highway Administration, 1972), 169
Maps, Catonsville (population distribution, 1910), 71-72
Maps, Catonsville (Sanborn, 1910), 65-70, 108, 121
Maps, Catonsville (Sanborn, 1925), 73-77, 125-126
Maps, Catonsville (Sanborn, 1930), 78-80, 127-129
Marsden, Joshuah, 34
Masonic Temple, 61, 97
McKinley, William, 28
Medicus, Mr. and Mrs. Howard, 165
Miller, Alfred J., "Election Scene at Catonsville," 14
Mohler, Donald I. and Emile R., homebuilders, 13, 123, 129, 138-146
Mohler, Frank L., Sr., and family, 123, 138-139
Morning Star Baptist Church, 128
Morsberger, Louis, 141
Mt. de Sales Academy, 146, 153
Mt. Olivet Methodist Church, 121, 128
Mt. St. Joseph's College High School, 164

N

National Recovery Administration, 124, 137
Newburg Hall, 18

O

Oak Forest Park, 13, 61, 104-105, 128
O'Conor, Piper and Flynn Realtors, 166
Occupations, Catonsville, 1880, 26
Occupations, Catonsville, 1910, 82-83, 89
Odd Fellows Hall (Ingleside Avenue), 114
Odd Fellows Hall (Winters Lane), 128
Old Corner Store (Frederick and Ingleside), 34, 166
Owens' Store (Library Hall), 101

P

Patapsco Light Company, 39
Parish, Mary, 153
Peach, Victorine, 153
Peregoy, John, and family, 63, 81, 100
Perkins, D. B., *Picturesque Catonsville*, 28
Pfeiffer family, 86
Pittroff, Mrs. E. L., 156
Plymouth Wallpaper Company, 12
Population, Catonsville, 13, 26, 63-64, 71-72, 81, 88-90, 92, 123-124, 127
Post Office, Catonsville, 31, 97
Pot and Kettle Club, 27, 115

R

Raab, F. C., Jr., 157
Raab, Michael and family, 25
Railroad Hotel, 12-13, 35-36, 129, 131
Read, Leo, 165
Reich, Esther, 154
Reich, Jake, 114
Reich's farm (Ingleside Avenue), 84
Rolling Road, 15
Rolling Road Golf Club, 59, 159
Ruff, "Shorty," 114
Russell's, Ltd., Restaurant, 37

S

St. Agnes Catholic Church, 12
St. Mark Catholic Church, 12, 24, 147
St. Mark Parish School, 62, 91, 111
St. Timothy's Episcopal Church, 12, 16, 50
St. Timothy's Hall, 16
Salem Lutheran Church, 12, 18, 24, 61, 97
Salem Lutheran Church, Ladies' Aid Society, 154
Scharf, J. Thomas, *History of Baltimore City and County*, 21, 27
Schatz Brothers, homebuilders, 118
Schon, Carl and George, 41
School Board, Baltimore County, 46, 59
Shepherd's Place Bookstore, 36
Shockett's Store (Edmondson Avenue and Winters Lane), 121
Smith, Albert (office), 36
Smith, George Jerome, 46
Smith, Harriet, 46
Somerset Group Homes, 138, 146
Standard Oil Service Station, (Frederick Road), 133
Steffens, Ann Loretta (Harmon), 164
Steffens, Walter J., 164
Sterling Ashton Funeral Home, 24
Stoddard, James, 37
Streetcars, streetcar electric lines, 16, 21, 24, 36, 39, 60, 94, 96, 101, 105, 122, 124, 146, 168
Sucro, George A., and family, 40-41
Summit (residence), 12, 28-29, 123, 138, 141-142
Summit Nursing Home, 138
Summit Park, 123, 138-142
Suter, H. Clay, 105
Suter Field, 113, 155

T

Ten Hills, 61, 105
Terminal Hotel, 16, 36-37, 122

U

Unger, John, 34
Union Trust Bank, Catonsville Branch, 124
University of Maryland Baltimore County, 168

W

Wacker, Charles and family, 41, 44-45, 51
Wagner, Emily, 154
Waldeck (residence), 24
Werner, Lena, 154
Westview Shopping Center, 116
Whitney's Meat Market, 12, 32
Wilkinson, Mary, 153
Williams, Dorsey W., 55
Williams' Store (Edmondson Avenue and Winters Lane), 121
Wilson, John S., 34
Wilson, John S., Lumber Company, 12, 30-31, 125, 127, 129, 135
Winters Lane (section of Catonsville), 24-25, 62, 71, 107, 121, 123, 128
Women's Christian Temperance Union (at Catonsville), 18
Women's Civic League of Catonsville, 62, 150
Wysham brothers, 34

About the Authors

Edward Orser and Joseph Arnold on Frederick Road in the heart of Catonsville.   Photo by Keith Weller, Catonsville Times

Drs. Edward Orser and Joseph Arnold are faculty members at the University of Maryland Baltimore County in Catonsville, Maryland.

Dr. Orser, associate professor and chairperson of the American Studies Department, earned his Ph.D. from the University of New Mexico and has taught at UMBC since 1969. His courses include Community in American Culture and Studies in Baltimore Society and Culture. His recent research on racial change in the Edmondson Village area of west Baltimore has been published in articles in the *Maryland Historical Magazine* and the *Journal of Urban History*. He also is the author of *Searching for a Viable Alternative: The Macedonia Cooperative Community, 1937-1958* (1981), the history of an experimental community in rural Georgia, and several articles on the social attitudes of the Protestant churches during World War II.

Dr. Arnold, professor of History, received his Ph.D. from Ohio State University and has taught at UMBC for twenty-one years. He specializes in the area of urban history, teaching courses on the development of cities in the United States. He is the author of several books and articles dealing with communities and neighborhoods in Maryland. In addition to his interest in urban and community history, Dr. Arnold has written two books on the history of water resource planning, *The Baltimore Engineers and the Chesapeake Bay* (1987) and *The Evolution of the Flood Control Act of 1936* (1988). Currently, Dr. Arnold is completing a book on Baltimore City in the years 1877 to 1904.

The two professors directed the research project and exhibit, "Catonsville, 1880-1940: From Village to Suburb," which included participation by ten undergraduate and graduate students from UMBC. The exhibit drew enthusiastic community audiences during August through September 1988 at UMBC's Albin O. Kuhn Library and Gallery and during December 1988 through February 1989 at the Catonsville Area Branch of the Baltimore County Public Library. Earlier UMBC Community Studies Projects have been on Irvington and on Gwynns Falls and Leakin Parks.

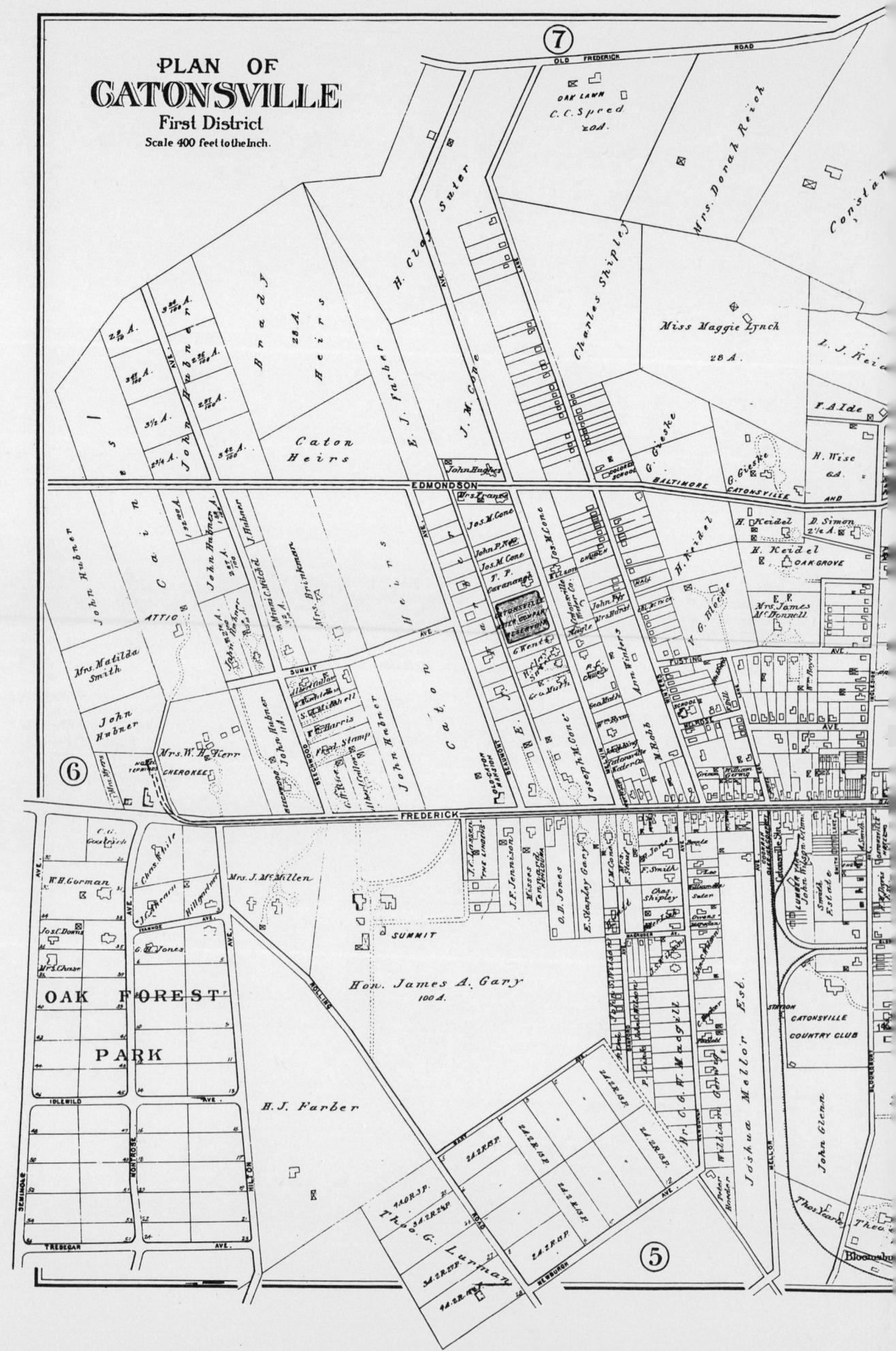